as much as,
IF NOT MORE THAN

ALSO BY H. L. HIX

* Also published by Etruscan Press

as much as,
IF NOT MORE THAN

H. L. HIX

etruscan press

Etruscan Press
Wilkes University
84 West South Street
Wilkes-Barre, PA 18766
(570) 408-4546

WILKES UNIVERSITY

www.etruscanpress.org

Published 2014 by Etruscan Press
Printed in the United States of America
Cover design by Carey Schwartzburt
Interior design by Julianne Popovec
The text of this book is set in Adobe Caslon Pro

First Edition

14 15 16 17 18 5 4 3 2 1

Library of Congress Cataloging-in-Publication Data

Hix, H. L.
  [Poems. Selections]
  As much as, if not more than / H. L. Hix.
     pages cm
  ISBN 978-0-9886922-1-3 (alk. paper)
  I. Title.
  PS3558.I88A83 2014
  811'.54--dc23
                                    2013042213

Please turn to the back of this book for a list of the sustaining funders of Etruscan Press.

as much as,
IF NOT MORE THAN

HARDEST STATEMENTS

Speechsung

Greek poets and dramatists sometimes employed a meter they called *logaoedic*, a term compounded of *logos*, meaning *speech*, and *aoide*, meaning *song*. Though not logaoedic in letter, since it does not consist, as did Greek logaoedic verse, in combining dactyls with trochees or anapests with iambs, the work that follows is logaoedic in spirit, at least in haunting the territory between speaking and singing, elenchus and jive.

If it claims logaoedic verse as a technical predecessor, the work that follows claims as one generic predecessor the "artist statement." Presented in connection with a visual art exhibition, the most provocative artist statements are themselves works of art. Simultaneously describing the work and compensating for it, the artist statement has both an expository aspect (here, viewer, is what you are seeing) and a counterfactual aspect (this, comrade, is what I would have made if only), and by analogy with such statements the works that follow seek to *ask after* and to *think through*.

Verse Points, Talking Points

The Ashmolean Museum houses a limestone ostracon "inscribed," the accompanying placard explains, "in hieratic by the scribe Amennakht with two poems composed by him." The inscription features periodic red dots above the lines, which the accompanying description identifies as "verse points," used, it says, "to indicate rhythmic units in literary texts," by analogy with line breaks. With concessions to limitations of contemporary technology (I have placed my verse points above *and beside* letters, rather than immediately above them, and I have not asked the publisher to incur the extra expense of having them printed in red), I have borrowed the technique of verse points and employed it in "More Than." For the stanza strings, I bear all blame.

"More Than" continues a dialogue that began as interviews, themselves collected in another volume, *Alter Nation* (Ugly Duckling Presse, 2013), which gives a bibliography of the books that occasioned them. Here, I wish simply to thank the following persons for their willingness to engage in such dialogue: Ali Alizadeh, Dan Beachy-Quick, Sherwin Bitsui, Rebecca Black, Shane Book, Jericho Brown, Astrid Cabral, Julie Carr, Jennifer Chang, Justin Chin, Don Mee Choi, Allison Adelle Hedge Coke, Mary Dalton, Sesshu Foster, Santee Frazier, Asher Ghaffar, Ferial Ghazoul, Johannes Göransson, Noah Eli Gordon, Kimiko Hahn, Sam Hamill, Robert Hass, Juan Felipe Herrera, Yunte Huang, Geof Huth, Gabriela Jauregui, Andrew Joron, Fady Joudah, Katia Kapovich, David Keplinger, Emelihter Kihleng, Peter H. Lee, Raina J. León, Alexis Levitin, Maurice Manning, Brandy Nalani McDougall, George Messo, Philip Metres, Dunya Mikhail, Wayne Miller, Chelsey Minnis, Rachel Moritz, Anna Moschovakis, Jennifer Moxley, Eileen Myles, Majid Naficy, Jesse Nathan, Uche Nduka, Idra Novey, Maggie Nelson, Mark Nowak, dg nanouk okpik, Danielle Pafunda, Sarith Peou, Craig Santos Perez, Mahealani Perez-Wendt, Jessica Piazza, Khadijah Queen, Sina Queyras, Mani Rao, Jed Rasula, Bino Realuyo, Barbara Jane Reyes, Ed Roberson, F. Daniel Rzicznek, Robyn Schiff, Susan Schultz, Ravi Shankar, Prageeta Sharma, Abraham Smith, Hazel Smith, Patricia Smith, Stephanie Strickland, Susan Tichy, Lyrae Van Clief-Stefanon, Meg Withers,

Rita Wong, Carolyne Wright, Jake Adam York, Linda Stern Zisquit. Except for those in "Self-Interview," the items gathered into "More Than" appear, in different versions, connected to rather than abstracted from their originating context, in *Alter Nation*.

Following Sources

The questions in "Self-Interview" have been hijacked from the following sources: Hannah Arendt, *Essays in Understanding: 1930-1954*; Gaston Bachelard, *The Poetics of Space*; Alain Badiou, *Logics of Worlds*; Alain Badiou, *Theory of the Subject*; Annette C. Baier, *Moral Prejudices*; Djuna Barnes, *Nightwood*; Georges Bataille, *Inner Experience*; Robert Browning, "Caliban Upon Setebos"; Judith Butler, *Giving an Account of Oneself*; Elias Canetti, *The Human Province*; Elias Canetti, *Notes from Hampstead*; Anne Carson, *Economy of the Unlost*; Anne Carson, *Eros the Bittersweet*; Dan Chiasson, *One Kind of Everything*; Hélène Cixous, *Stigmata* ; J. M. Coetzee, *In the Heart of the Country*; Gilles Deleuze, *Difference and Repetition*; Denis Diderot, *D'Alembert's Dream*; George Eliot, *Silas Marner*; T. S. Eliot, *The Waste Land*; Maud Ellmann, *The Hunger Artists*; Clayton Eshleman, *Companion Spider*; Louise Glück, *Meadowlands*; William Goyen, *House of Breath*; Kate Greenstreet, *Case Sensitive*; Kate Greenstreet, *The Last 4 Things*; Abdulrazak Gurnah, *Paradise*; Lars Gustafsson, *The Death of a Beekeeper*; Donna J. Haraway, *Simians, Cyborgs, and Women*; Martin Heidegger, *Being and Time*; Lyn Hejinian, *Saga/Circus*; Eric Hoffer, Notebooks; Susan Howe, *My Emily Dickinson*; Luce Irigaray, *This Sex Which Is Not One*; Carol Jacobs, *Skirting the Ethical*; Barbara Johnson, *The Critical Difference*; Edward P. Jones, *All Aunt Hagar's Children*; Edward P. Jones, *The Known World*; John Keats, "Ode to a Nightingale"; Frieda Knobloch, *Botanical Companions*; Julia Kristeva, *Desire in Language*; Stefanie Marlis, *Cloudlife*; Carole Maso, *Ghost Dance* ; Lynne McFall, *The One True Story of the World*; Heather McHugh, *Broken English*; Anne Michaels, *Fugitive Pieces*; Czeslaw Milosz, *Emperor of the Earth*; Toni Morrison, *Beloved*; Toni Morrison, *Sula*; Toni Morrison, *Tar Baby*; Nicholas Mosley, *Hopeful Monsters*; Nicholas Mosley, *Serpent*; Iris Murdoch, *Metaphysics as a Guide to Morals*; Iris Murdoch, *Nuns and Soldiers*; Martin Andersen Nexø, *Pelle the Conqueror*; Friedrich Nietzsche, *The Antichrist*; Kate Northrop, *Back Through Interruption*; Martha C. Nussbaum, *The Fragility of Goodness*; Martha C. Nussbaum, *Love's Knowledge*; George Oppen, *Selected Prose, Daybooks, and Papers*; José Ortega y Gasset, *The Dehumanization of Art*; Alice Oswald, *Dart*; Octavio Paz, *Convergences*; Antonio Porchia, *Voices*; Lia Purpura, *Increase* ;

Carl Rakosi, *Collected Prose*; Adrienne Rich, *Arts of the Possible*; Jacqueline Risset, *Sleep's Powers*; Marilynne Robinson, *Housekeeping*; Cristina Peri Rossi, *State of Exile*; Jean-Jacques Rousseau, *Discourse on Inequality*; Arundhati Roy, *The God of Small Things*; Salman Rushdie, *Midnight's Children*; Nawal El Saadawi, *The Fall of the Imam*; Sherod Santos, *A Poetry of Two Minds*; James Scully, *Line Break*; Michel Serres, *Malfeasance*; William Shakespeare, *King Lear*; William Shakespeare, *The Tempest*; William Shakespeare, *Titus Andronicus*; Johanna Skibsrud, *I Do Not Think That I Could Love a Human Being*; Ahdaf Soueif, *The Map of Love*; Susan Stewart, *Poetry and the Fate of the Senses*; Peter Szendy, *Prophecies of Leviathan*; Wang Ping, *The Magic Whip*; Brad Watson, *Aliens in the Prime of Their Lives*; Zoë Wicomb, *David's Story* ; Joy Williams, *The Quick and the Dead*; William Carlos Williams, "Portrait of a Lady"; Christian Wiman, *Ambition and Survival*; Jeanette Winterson, *Art [Objects]*; Ludwig Wittgenstein *Culture and Value*; Ludwig Wittgenstein, *On Certainty*; Ludwig Wittgenstein, *Remarks on Colour*; Ludwig Wittgenstein, *Zettel*.

In each case, the "asking" question comes from a source written by a male, and the "answering" question from a source written by a female.

Incited

Though otherwise they follow their chosen form, the glosa, the poems in "As Much As" eschew the customary presentation of their quoted lines first as epigraphs. Instead, they invite the reader to the sources' source: a project called "Show and Tell," archived at www.hlhix.com (click on the red IN QUIRE button, and then on the "Show and Tell" button), in which writers respond lyrically, rather than critically, to work by artists. The poems do not demand, but do welcome, the reader's acquaintance with those conversations, which they join in progress, pursuing (whether or not they *achieve*) a kind of thinking that can occur only in, and as, dialogue. Each glosa responds to one artist/writer pairing. In each glosa, the last lines of the first and second stanzas quote the artist, and the last lines of the third and fourth stanzas quote the writer.

I am grateful to the following artists and writers for conversing in a forum that allows the rest of us to listen in, and that incited me to respond: Daniel Dove & Ann McCutchan; Gerry Trilling & Nin Andrews; Phillip Michael Hook & Matthew Cooperman; Thomas Lyon Mills & Evie Shockley; Cassandra Hooper & Alyson Hagy; Alisa Henriquez & Caleb Klaces; Bruce Checefsky & Mary Quade; Vera Scekic & Jericho Brown; Christopher Leitch & Supriya Bhatnagar; Jane Lackey & Carol Moldaw; Anne Devaney & Jonathan Weinert; Leeah Joo & Jennifer Atkinson; Mark Ritchie & Walter Cummins; Leah Hardy & Christine Gelineau; Susan Moldenhauer & Bruce Bond; Sarah Walko & Bin Ramke; Sreshta Rit Premnath & Debra Di Blasi; Anne Lindberg & Renée Ashley; Jason Dodge & Philip Metres; Shelby Shadwell & Alison Calder; Aviva Rahmani & Rupert Loydell; Doug Russell & Andrew Joron; Susan Bee & Patty Seyburn; Brian Dupont & Rita Wong; China Marks & Denise Duhamel; Garry Noland & Jonathan Farmer; Anna Von Mertens & Afaa Michael Weaver; Murat Germen & Nina Foxx; Katherine Mann & Anis Shivani; Adriane Herman & Laura Mullen; Judi Ross & Erin Murphy; Christine Drake & Cynthia Atkins; John Ferry & Peter Jay Shippy; Ien Dobbelaar & Michelle Boisseau; Jim Sajovic & Susan Aizenberg; David Jouris & Michael Waters; Etsuko Ichikawa & Thomas E. Kennedy.

Privilege, Blessings, Grace

The epigraph to "More Than" is from Theodor Adorno, *Minima Moralia*. The epigraph to "As Much As" is from Luce Irigaray, *Elemental Passions*.

Versions of several of the pieces that together comprise this book have enjoyed the privilege of prior separate publication (often under different titles), for which I am grateful to the editors of the following journals: *Alabama Literary Review, Bat City Review, Cimarron Review, High Desert Journal, I-70 Review, Kenyon Review, Michigan Quarterly Review, The Kokanee, North American Review, Numero Cinq, Open Window Review, Rampike, Taos Journal of Poetry & Art, Unsplendid, Virginia Quarterly Review, Zone 3.*

A portion of "Neither Plea of Innocence Nor Admission of Guilt" was published in *The Tower of Babel*, ed. Rupert Loydell (Like This Press, 2013).

This book assumed something like its final form during a residency at the Anderson Center. For the focused time given me by that residency, I am in debt to the Center, and especially to its Director, Robert Hedin. That residency occurred during a sabbatical leave from the University of Wyoming. For the blessing of a full year in which to pursue research and writing without other job responsibilities, I am grateful to the University.

It seems almost trivializing to note Kate Northrop's support for this particular work, inseparable as that support is from her ongoing, comprehensive grace. A statement of thanks ought to be made in public, but in this matter thanks is subsumed by love, declarations of which belong in private. You see my dilemma.

MORE THAN

No more than it is spirits who send the dream,
is it the ego that dreams.

DEFINITIONS

Written on, and writing.
Events mistaken for conditions. °
° Pretense of one-to-one ratio,˙ anecdote to
epiphany. °
° ° ° ° ° ° ° The Constitution that constitutes˙ what precedes any constitution.
° °

Willing suspension of *any*˙ constituent of sound judgment. ° ° ° ° ° ° ° ° ° ° °
° Household gods
fed through diaspora,˙ while one's children go hungry. ° ° ° ° ° ° ° ° ° ° ° °
° Scheming on the
loading dock about˙ the scheming at the conference table. ° ° ° ° ° ° ° ° ° ° °
° The difference
between what arrived˙ and whatever what was already there˙ when what
arrived arrived was waiting for. °
° Labor's idle chatter, interrupting˙ idleness's
labors. °
° ° ° ° ° *Civis*, dreaming itself *animus*.

Written over, in all the ways one might mean that.
This darkness, not *any*. °
° ° ° ° ° ° ° ° ° ° ° ° ° ° ° Not emotion but clarity,˙ not recollected but pursued,˙
not in tranquility but from dis-ease. °
° The home reason ran from, but will be˙
beggared back to. °
° ° ° ° ° ° ° ° ° ° ° ° Prophetic then, now nostalgic. ° ° ° ° ° ° ° ° ° ° ° ° ° ° ° ° ° ° °
° Not arguments for
immortality,˙ but demonstrations of *post*˙mortality, *a*mortality. ° ° ° ° ° ° ° ° ° °
° The reality of
unreality. °
° ° ° ° ° ° Voice that precedes its speaker. °
° Vision loaned to vision made. ° ° ° ° ° °
° A map
of sonic entanglements laid over˙ a map of conceptual entanglements.˙ The
spaces defined by their non-coincidence.

The sufficiency unto us of the sufficient unto itself.
Mosaic vista onto the land˙ both promised and forbidden. ° ° ° ° ° ° ° ° ° ° °
° Words separable˙
but not separate˙ from memories. °
° Mediated alertness˙ to immediacy. ° ° ° ° ° ° ° °
° A qualified
testament˙ to the unqualified. °
° ° ° ° ° ° ° ° ° ° ° ° ° ° ° ° ° ° ° *Wary,* become *weary.* ° ° ° ° ° ° ° ° ° ° ° ° ° ° ° ° °
° Given: *x is y.* Understood:˙
what a life might be like if x were y. °
° The Romeo-and-Juliet longing˙ of words
and sensations, desperate˙ less because their love is futile (though it is)˙ than
because they themselves are foolish. °
° Self-collection. ° ° ° ° ° ° ° ° ° ° ° ° ° ° ° °
° The rickety wooden chair˙
on its side in the back of the attic˙ when you moved in, and when you move
out.

As if it weren't compensatory.
Language's elegy,˙ taken for one's own. °
° Capitulation of categorical˙ to
hypothetical. °
° ° ° ° ° ° ° ° ° If the recto of imperative˙ is mandate, the verso. ° ° ° ° ° ° ° ° ° ° °
° Works cited.
° °

Surveillance against surveillance. Though our seeing˙ be always overseen,
seeing as if˙ it were not. °
° ° ° ° ° ° ° ° ° ° ° ° ° ° ° ° A measuring of distance˙ from the scene, the event.
° °

Any bridge from mythic to here. °
° The limits desire and language˙ impose each
on the other. °
° ° ° ° ° ° ° ° ° Wavelengths we cannot see,˙ influencing what we can.

8

Leaning on a mop, looking out a window at the weather.
Subject without predicate. °
° ° ° ° ° ° ° ° ° ° ° ° ° ° ° ° ° ° The making plausible of what can't˙ be rationalized,
the rationalizing˙ of what can't be made plausible. °
° Consciousness melted,
leaving (like lost wax)˙ the shape of rationality but not˙ its substance.
° °

Mimesis, but not˙ of objects in the world. °
° Finality from which˙ we yet may
find release. °
° ° ° ° ° ° ° ° One finality, as preparation˙ for the impossible next. ° ° ° ° ° ° ° ° ° °
° Deference of
singularity and finality˙ to triviality and fungibility. ° ° ° ° ° ° ° ° ° ° ° ° ° ° ° ° ° ° °
° *Seeking* absence and
invisibility,˙ as if one were not possessed of them already. ° ° ° ° ° ° ° ° ° ° ° ° ° °
° The wish that the
center hold,˙ absent any belief that it could.

The difference between what I am called *and what I am* named. Staring into the sun anyway. ° Reverence the vice,˙ irreverence the virtue. °

After learning one's place˙ but before taking it. ° *Lingering,* chosen over˙ destination. Pilgrim's pauses. ° Progression, where progress is inconceivable. °

An answer to "Why *this* list?" ° Not the *operation* but the *fact*˙ of the metaphysical. ° Notes taken as one takes a punch. ° The absurd fact˙ that the facts out-absurd˙ absurdity itself.

Renaming, not rebirth.

Quick, into the cellar! But˙ we have no cellar. °
° *Embrace me, my love!*, pled˙ not
to the mirror but to empty air. °
° ° ° ° ° ° ° ° ° ° ° ° ° ° ° ° ° ° Final, not provisional, separation˙ of intention
from action. °
° ° ° ° ° ° ° ° ° As if ambiguity˙ were clarity. Because˙ ambiguity *is* clarity.
° °

Justified false belief. °
° ° ° ° ° ° ° ° ° ° ° Restoration of ideals˙ to the problems their adoption˙
purports to overcome. °
° ° ° ° ° ° ° ° ° ° ° ° ° ° ° ° ° *Anti*-epiphany. °
° The point of equal focus for˙ advancing
image and retreating. °
° ° ° ° ° ° ° ° ° ° ° ° ° The greeting arriving image˙ and departing image
exchange.

Preference, in the absence of choice.

Sonic madness. °

° ° ° ° ° ° ° ° ° ° ° The tittering of a plastic straw˙ struck by bicycle spokes. ° ° ° ° ° °

° A

second conversation, without a first. °

° What begins in wonder˙ and *stays* there.

° °

What cries for justice. What justice cries for. °

° The wounds inflicted one on

the other˙ by a creature with a skeleton˙ and a creature without, mating. ° ° °

° The

perfect circle inscribed by a mule˙ tethered to a stake. ° ° ° ° ° ° ° ° ° ° ° ° ° ° ° ° °

° Chickens pecking at the

dust˙ around the House of Cultural Prestige. °

° Bustle in the City of Loneliness.

For absent external markers, compensatory internal ones.
Loves, taxonomized according to˙ what element of the ideal each lacks.

Pointing at what cannot be named,˙ naming what cannot be pointed at. ˚ ˚ ˚
A
lexicon of scraps,˙ a grammar of their placement. ˚ ˚ ˚ ˚ ˚ ˚ ˚ ˚ ˚ ˚ ˚ ˚ ˚ ˚ ˚ ˚
Continuing reassignment˙
to memory of its significance. ˚
Complexity seen through rather than seen.
On behalf of a reclusive ultimacy. ˚ ˚ ˚ ˚ ˚ ˚ ˚ ˚ ˚ ˚ ˚ ˚ ˚ ˚ ˚ ˚ ˚ ˚ ˚
Because we have not achieved reason.˙
Until we do. ˚
Tribal lord, in the treacherous terrain˙ between fact and truth.

Better Cassandra˙ than Achilles.

CRITERIA

To recognize as consequential *the forms of things.*
To collect and arrange what had been dispersed. Not make *up*, but make
plain. In preference to anecdote, testimony; to introspection, research; to
disinterestedness, advocacy. *Collective* tranquility, not individual, as the
condition of wholesome recollection. Keep the rule, leave me the exception.

"But it's a 'people issue' to *me!*" To make myself more fully what I *am not* than
what I *am.* To prefer desperate hope to confident hope. False, but not
misleading. Unacknowledged legislator, my ass. Unacknowledged insurgent,
you mean.

To seek instances, *not only* objects.
To bear the weight of history, though none˙ can bear up under it.

Definition, not the word defined. Not the solution˙ to an equation or the object˙ of a proof, but the iteration˙ of a function. Not endpoint,˙ but progress. "I reckon." You wish. With so few willing to address˙ argument and evidence,˙ reason needs *something* to do. Always already compromised,˙ never compromising. When did you last have a plausible dream?˙ A plausible premonition? Because *thinking* belongs to grief, too. Because I can better discern˙ what my obligations *would be*˙ than what they are.

To worry *each step in a progress.*

I knew that already. Did you have to remind me? Not persona, a sounding-through, but perfacia, an acting-through. Not that one says what one says through the mask, but that one sees what one sees and does what one does.

Curious about the carious, careful of the hollowed-out. Present to the absent.

Because *how* what is said is said matters to the polis as much as what is said.

To beg for change, then curse the one who offers it. Not to *consolidate* the past, but to *liberate* it. To make it not more solid, but less.

Pursue fidelity to its extreme; uphold fidelity in extremity. There it waits, whether we have run from it or toward it, whether we fear it or embrace it.

Maybe it's important that we *not* name those from whom a name has been taken.

To take onto oneself the bending.
To move more slowly, to see˙ at a different pace, making˙ others' later travel safer. ˚
˚ ˚ ˚ As immeasurable as the sea,˙ as full of mysteries and monsters. ˚ ˚ ˚ ˚ ˚ ˚ ˚ ˚
˚ Not to distinguish platitude˙ from truth, but to find solace˙ in their indistinguishability. ˚
˚ ˚ ˚ ˚ ˚ ˚ ˚ ˚ ˚ ˚ ˚ ˚ More real than we can comprehend,˙ less real than we can believe. ˚
˚ ˚ ˚ ˚ ˚ ˚ ˚ ˚ To guess what has been guessed. ˚ ˚ ˚ ˚ ˚ ˚ ˚ ˚ ˚ ˚ ˚ ˚ ˚ ˚ ˚ ˚ ˚ ˚ ˚
˚ Was that *Farewell* or *Welcome*?
˚ ˚

Lead me, lost one. ˚
˚ ˚ ˚ ˚ ˚ ˚ ˚ ˚ ˚ ˚ ˚ ˚ Rationalized, eroticized. Same thing. ˚ ˚ ˚ ˚ ˚ ˚ ˚ ˚ ˚ ˚ ˚ ˚ ˚
˚ Beyond the world in which reactions˙ are equal and opposite. Hang on.

To accept that there are, but not to accept, limits to language.
To true the relationship· between death and hope. ° ° ° ° ° ° ° ° ° ° ° ° ° ° ° ° ° °
° Instead of the Instead Of.
° °

Constellated, in daylight. °
° ° ° ° ° ° ° ° ° ° ° ° ° ° ° ° ° ° Detachment indistinguishable from immersion.
° °

To contain the backstory· *and* reveal it. °
° Even in this country whose language·
I cannot understand and whose god· I do not know, I recognize this voice·
as a call to prayer, and I answer it. °
° Not to charge percepts with symbolic
power,· but to draw on power with which· they already were charged. ° ° ° ° °
° Is this
the pathetic fallacy?· Or is my grief unbounded? ° ° ° ° ° ° ° ° ° ° ° ° ° ° ° ° ° °
° Down, you hit bottom.· Up,
you never stop.

To pardon being and *to petition it for pardon.*
Urged by words to eschew words. °°°°°°°°°°°°°°°°°°°°°°°°°°°°°°°°°°
°°°°°°°°°°°°°°°°°°°°°°°°°°°° "Don't *say* that." °°°°°°°°°°°°°°°°°°°°°
°°°°°°°°°°°°°°°°°°°°°°°°°°°°°°°° Two neighbors talking over
a fence.° Some work is not getting done. Some is. °°°°°°°°°°°°°°°°
°°°°°°°°°°°°°°°°°°°°°°°°°°°°°°°°° Why not language play as
sex play? °°
°°°°°° My body with your body.° My voice with yours. °°°°°°°°°°°°
°°°°°°°°°°°°°°°°°°°°°°°°°°°°°°°°°°°°°° To know otherwise:
to know° through a different means, and to know° a contrary to be true.

°°
Intransitivity: waiting,° without waiting for. °°°°°°°°°°°°°°°°°°°°
°°°°°°°°°°°°°°°°°°°°°°°°°°°°° Flight, used to return to the coop.
°°

How rich can my soul be° if my neighborhood's poor?° How rich, if it's
rich?

To separate the conditions by *which one lives from those* in *which one lives.* Knowledge unsettled, knowledge bound. ° Neither secrecy nor silence, but bounded by both. ° If only nature were civil. If only we were. ° Choose one if you want. I listen for god *and* the devil. ° Myth, memory external to the poet; history, memory still internal. ° A real person's real life can be also archetypal, a Sartrean, Dantesque hell. ° To immerse oneself in place and time, to free oneself from place and time. To *get immersed.* ° Here mountain bluebirds hover over glacier-glazed stones, but *any* boundary between natural and supernatural hosts emissaries peculiar to that place. ° Identity fixed by boundaries, boundaries by identity.

To release reason from, even oppose it to, obligation. With fluency if possible, without if necessary. Because we are *vulnerable to the truth.* To *speak of* a story but withhold the story itself. Intransitivity: to search, but not search *for.* I'm not grieving the loss of someone, I'm just grieving. Grief remarking not the lost loved one, but itself. I have no *cause* for my grief, any more than for my joy. Though there be no feeling better, yet may there be feeling with. The law and human dignity are not coextensive, and *something* needs to fulfill the terms of dignity.

To name what arises in this world for what passes over it.
To create, record, remember to ourselves˙ the *we*-ness of the *we*, the
even distribution˙ of humanity that forever contests˙ the radically uneven
distribution˙ of pain, suffering, and violence. ˙
˙ Not what the world is like, just
how to get˙ from one word to the next. ˙
˙ Return, repressed. Return, return.
˙ ˙

Under the reign of corruption,˙ *analytical* skill conditions˙ the possibility of
resistance.˙ I can't resist a lie I can't identify. ˙ ˙ ˙ ˙ ˙ ˙ ˙ ˙ ˙ ˙ ˙ ˙ ˙ ˙ ˙ ˙ ˙ ˙ ˙
˙ To move, not geographical
location˙ but epistemological location. ˙
˙ Not consolation but convocation.
˙ ˙

Like photographing tattoos:˙ to record how (and how indelibly)˙ we are
marked. ˙
˙ ˙ ˙ ˙ ˙ ˙ How *well* you take it down may not be˙ identical to, but will depend
on,˙ how *accurately*. ˙
˙ ˙ ˙ ˙ ˙ ˙ ˙ ˙ ˙ ˙ ˙ ˙ To see, warily. The hard-edged,˙ high-stakes wariness
with which˙ one flushes when encountering˙ a stranger on an otherwise˙
abandoned street late at night.

THRUSTS

Even God must be curious about this. Labor matters more to ideas˙ than ideas to labor. The more securely the ring holds it,˙ the less brightly will the diamond˙ glimmer and shine. Loves, after all, do not replace,˙ but complement, one another. Poetry's not arousing empathy˙ in the same ways that other language uses do˙ might be for some less problematic than˙ its not offering *avoidance* in the same ways. In the space of exchange, well-being˙ follows increase and accumulation;˙ in the space of decision, it follows˙ deliberation, the sustaining of˙ an array of possible realities. The same smug piety that corrupts˙ the religious and the patriotic˙ also corrupts us, the self-proclaimed poets. Cast out of poetry, cast out˙ of civil society. The homeland in which I would be at home,˙ not the one in which I live. The spoken is not made true by the truth˙ of what it speaks *of*; the truth of the true˙ arises from its spokenness.

Take note(s).

If fiction records the marriage,˙ lyric anticipates its failure. ˚ ˚ ˚ ˚ ˚ ˚ ˚ ˚ ˚ ˚ ˚ ˚ ˚
˚ Narrative
identification:˙ seeing myself as someone else˙ shows me I am not who I
thought I was.˙ Lyric identification:˙ seeing the world as something else˙
shows me I am not where I thought I was. ˚
˚ To see the other : to see *as* the
other. ˚
˚ ˚ ˚ ˚ The pastoral, from a riding lawnmower.˙ Shelley's skylark, one
hypocrisy˙ of the middle class. ˚
˚ ˚ ˚ ˚ ˚ ˚ ˚ ˚ ˚ ˚ ˚ ˚ ˚ ˚ ˚ ˚ ˚ ˚ The pattern that antedates the poem˙ funds
both the poem's truth and its falsity. ˚
˚ The run-on: *just get it said.*
˚ ˚

Complicity in colonialism˙ does not oblige one to its enforcement
mechanisms. ˚
˚ ˚ ˚ ˚ ˚ ˚ ˚ ˚ Synthesizing information˙ may not be our only charge;˙ what
about reiterating it,˙ or recontextualizing it? ˚ ˚ ˚ ˚ ˚ ˚ ˚ ˚ ˚ ˚ ˚ ˚ ˚ ˚ ˚ ˚ ˚
˚ Colonialism: to the mines
with them,˙ or to the cane fields. Let the material˙ become ours. And the
poems, the poems.

Taken back already, even before I say it.
Descartes asserts, in principle˙ if not in practice, an end. Things sum˙ to a
total, so reality is substantial.˙ But if we regard things as recursive˙ rather
than cumulative, we find˙ a reality not substance but function.˙ We cannot
match the world, only˙ reiterate it. Or even match ourselves,˙ since we are
not self-identical. °
° ° ° ° ° ° ° ° ° ° ° Always memory and language want˙ reconciliation. Always
they need˙ a mediator. °
° ° ° ° ° ° ° ° ° ° ° ° ° Narrative reconciles words with events,˙ but at what
cost. Lyric's reconciliation˙ is no less Mephistophelean. ° ° ° ° ° ° ° ° ° ° ° ° ° °
° Poetry has in
common with pornography˙ shamelessness. At least. ° ° ° ° ° ° ° ° ° ° ° ° ° ° ° °
° Occasional, if not by
derivation˙ from some specific event, yet in˙ the Miltonian sense: "And by
occasion foretells…" °
° ° ° ° ° ° ° ° ° ° ° ° Decorative, not in the sense˙ of ornamentality, but as˙
connected etymologically˙ with "decent" and "dignity." ° ° ° ° ° ° ° ° ° ° ° ° ° ° °
° Counternarrative
not as a different˙ outcome of events but as complexity˙ in place of
oversimplification. °
° ° ° ° ° ° ° ° ° ° ° ° In "the war story," the enemy˙ always lies, always says
something I wouldn't.˙ The war story can speak *about*,˙ but never *as*, the
enemy. °
° ° ° ° ° Who does not long for faith˙ in the *efficacy* of form?˙ If I could find
order, chaos˙ would diminish in the face of it.

Events fugitive, memories insecure. So what?
Poetry makes nothing happen, yes, but what the hell. Nothing *needs* to
happen for something to change. Maybe for *everything* to change. One
tragedy of any tragedy: told, it stands for all the untold others. If I don't need
the *as if*, then poetry makes nothing happen. On the necessity of *as if*
rides the validity and worth of poetry. Make nothing happen: resist the
impulse to co-opt others' wills toward my ends. Poetry makes something *not*
happen. *Prophetic*, not by foreseeing a future that otherwise no one could
know in advance, but by declaring inevitabilities otherwise repressed or
denied. Insofar as sound choice of direction depends on accurate knowledge
of initial position, a poem's *locating* me is a service at once moral, political,
and practical. The double-nation of rich and poor in this double nation is
acknowledged because the rich can reconcile it with their moral views: in a
land that offered equal opportunity, economic standing would be earned,
and the wealthy would be virtuous, the poor vicious. But our other
double-nations, of race, for instance, remain underground. We see the grass
but not the soil.

The obvious is not obvious at all.
Everything archetypal, nothing particular. Each individual rather than representing the species *is* the species.
Because *someone* has to ask, about what "we" assume as "ours," what "it's ours" *means*, and how it came to *be* "ours," and what it *is* that is "ours."
The paradigmatic poem: a simple *listing* of the names of the dead.
A list need not be *given* purpose to *have* it.
The bluntest truths and sharpest pains may be the *least* dramatic.
Partiality as the hope for peace. Because man's inhumanity to man is perpetual, it can never *be* total.
One account establishes correspondences as plausible; another takes them for granted.
A name: the one miracle.
Only naming frees us to grieve. Only naming frees the spirit of the dead to depart.

Some questions are ruined by an answer.
At a certain level of self-consciousness,˙ the future tense will seem
dangerous.
If I'm the doer, I'm the done unto. The psychic literalizes˙ spirits the
poet figures. Better a dented spittoon at your feet˙ than a well-wrought urn
in a locked case. What is soft and porous of us hosts˙ our vulnerability and
our shame. Softened. Poor us. Documentation as understatement:˙ to allow
another to speak˙ for him- or herself, without gloss,˙ to trust both the
quoted person and the reader. To resist, I must first create conditions˙ in
which my resistance is not˙ preemptively erased or co-opted. That I don't
mean to be policing˙ anything does not put it in my power˙ *not* to police.

28

Untrue, but not trivial.
The trail of bread crumbs didn't lead Hansel and Gretel back, but did lead the sparrows forward. °
° ° ° ° ° ° ° ° ° ° ° ° ° What prevents me from thinking the poem has *done* the work it *invites*? °
° ° ° ° ° ° ° ° ° ° ° ° ° Even if one of two things seen is *not* real, the duality, the perception of both, *is*. °
° ° ° ° ° ° ° ° ° ° ° ° ° ° There is good haunting no less than bad. ° ° ° ° ° ° ° ° ° °
° The true never did coincide with the real. °
° ° ° ° ° ° ° ° ° ° ° ° ° ° ° ° ° Because there are true truths and false truths, false lies and true ones. The facts simpliciter never suffice. ° ° ° ° ° ° ° ° ° ° °
° Thinking about but not looking at the forbidden is one way to take seriously its forbiddenness. °
° ° ° ° ° ° ° ° ° ° "I" opposite "they" rather than opposite "he" or "she." ° ° ° ° ° ° °
° Who do I know by name, the servants or the masters? Who do I eat with? Well, then.

What the landscape cannot orient.
The capacity for *self-deception*, not for reason, sets us apart from other animals.
Unruliness as responsibility.
Even when it does not violate the rules, love still defies them.
Truth and beauty in spite of conditions, or in concord with conditions. To call both "poetry" is one lie of power.
Those with the most prominent platform have the most interest in believing those platforms impartial and their holders (themselves) godlike, a self-fulfilling prophecy at work in poetry as in politics.
The search for origins finds its satisfaction in myth, and myth its satisfaction in order. What are origins origins *of*, if not of order?
How strange, to *make* a mistake. How strange, that one might have reason to do so.
Sympathy: lamenting the conditions in which another lives, without *acting* to relieve those conditions.
What is *indeterminate* about an image, not what is *determinate*, conveys its meaning.

Not difficult to understand, *just difficult to* face up to. Seekers after peace *act* on the recognition that powerlessness is more to be desired than is power.

Critique need not be explicit to be critique. To imagine an alternative is to perform a critique.

What ought poetry lead to? What does it offer? What does it demand of me?

Monstrosity: the norm, not the exception.

Afraid of meaning too little, afraid of meaning too much. Taken down. Taken up. We who would be poets have to hope there really is division of labor.

Forms of incomprehension. Plural.

Some confines are more confining than others.

No materials for an ark, but a portent of deluge.

SELF-INTERVIEW

Why is it so hard to tell the truth?
How can the stakes in love and work be sorted out?

How can one learn the truth by thinking?
What must resemblance resemble?

And how does one pay for thoughts?
And where is the human store to which such goods are gathered?

What is the interior of the interior?
But where is *being* being kept?

Do you know the old man who hunts imaginary lions on the grounds?
Where's a person going to move if he's used to having lions?

Is it characteristic of "the beautiful" that it can never be seen again?
How can you stand it — *looking* at things?

How are *we to draw a demarcation line between a true Event and its semblance?*
What is the relation of impertinence to the hope of understanding?

About the dream, then?
In what form — spilled?

What do we really *want when we dirty the world?*
How is so much ordinary value thrown away?

Perhaps he was adrift on the last scrap of earth, and was the only person still living?
But how could I know unless I went there?

Who is the third who walks always beside you?
What voice when we hesitate and are silent is moving to meet us?

Was that an accident, fate, or providence?
Saved from what?

And then what? What tomorrow and the next day?
Over and over it comes round, as in a shooting gallery, a blue duck among
the yellow: where is home?

*How will they be, if we who are present do not blow life into them and create
them?*
Speaking this language, eating strange food, wearing these clothes?

But wherefore rough, why cold and ill at ease?
Who are you? What is the nature of your crime?

Revenge? Revenge?
But where does the flesh of the other begin?

What is a self, as distinct from a person?
Can the act of speaking have *one* subject?

And the other, was he there?
To perfectly hear oneself speak, shouldn't one listen from a distance as if to
a stranger?

Is there now too much grief for thought to handle?
Well there isn't, is there?

We will return to this place?
With its rag rug and wooden table?

Who would believe this hollow noise is the sea?
What are the social mechanisms for passing on rules for telling stories?

If you could escape from your sufferings, and did so, where would you go outside them?
If it hurts, why don't you cry?

If everything we touch and name becomes full of meaning, and if all these meanings — provisional, disparate, contradictory — instantly lose their meaning, what is left to us?
What we carry?

What really sets a limit to the space you feel you occupy? I mean the real sphere of your sensations?
What is it that anorectics cannot "swallow" if not the very words that brought about their illness in the first place?

What if the actual problem is not to bridge the gap but, rather, to formulate it as such, to conceive it properly?
And why has the rule about places being not too dark and not too light been combined with the one about memorising in quiet districts, to produce this mystical obscurity and retirement in which the *sensibilia* are unified and their underlying order perceived?

By whom, what hand?
Realize what you've just done?

Do you do more than what is allowed by God and the law?
And what if the wind had risen?

Is it also true that the more one subtracts the more luminous the thing becomes?
What might it mean to make an ethic from the region of the unwilled?

34

Which shore? Which shore?
What has happened to our lives?

If we pose the question of "world," which world is meant?
What is it that we are trying to go through? The space of the very act of naming?

What do you know about them apart from these stories about snakes and men eating metal?
Cannot a beastly thing be analogous to a fine thing if both are apprehensions?

Where shall we find the material to reconstruct the world?
How long does pity take?

What does it mean, after all, to have integrity *in matters of the spirit?*
Can't we be gentle first, and honest later?

Is my understanding only blindness to my own lack of understanding?
Have you any idea what goes into water?

Does one ever get used to living in a world like this?
How *do* they come back, these dead?

To what are we dedicated if not to those problems that demand the very transformation of our body and our language?
How much did your upbringing prepare you to acknowledge and respond to the voice of a stone or the generous help of a bird *in its language?*

In this drama of intimate geometry, where should one live?
In all the world?

What solace are lapidary paradoxes for the loves of the body?
Or had they started their lives as town trees?

Yet what does form *mean?*
Why be made to tremble and sob by the clouds?

What poetic universe does that imply?
What is exile like for you?

Was it a vision, or a waking dream?
Where have you been and when were you born and are you still alive?

Does it make it any better if we know these images come from our unconscious?
Kept the corona of her hair from unplaiting behind her in the breeze as she
bent to study the face of a flower or the jeweled back of a beetle in the sun?

Where there is no love, of what use is beauty?
What is the antidote to these stratagems?

When heaven doth weep, doth not the earth o'erflow?
Does it matter where the birds go?

Would it be correct to say our concepts reflect our life?
What did she see, as she looked into the glassy eye of the camera, that
frightened her so?

In such a night as this?
Might trust itself be pathological?

What if the inner life doesn't really exist?
I don't mind, do you?

Where should this music be?
At the center of what?

What is the maximum distance from which you can love a person?
Can love, in its last extremity, create its object?

The other endings?
What, can't we ever rest?

PARRIES

I belong to one world, but live in the other.
Problems as *events* invite˙ replacement by other events that fulfill˙ the system to more congenial effect;˙ problems as *symptoms* invite˙ alteration of the system.˙ Disguise vs. cure. ˚
˚ "Still": "quiet, unmoving"˙ or "yet, continuing." Why can "stillness"˙ develop only the former sense? ˚ ˚ ˚ ˚ ˚ ˚ ˚ ˚ ˚ ˚ ˚ ˚ ˚ ˚ ˚ ˚
˚ Imagination as civil disobedience:˙ to refuse existing constructions of duty˙ as a minion of obligation, electing˙ responsibility on other terms. ˚ ˚ ˚ ˚ ˚ ˚ ˚ ˚ ˚ ˚ ˚ ˚ ˚ ˚ ˚ ˚ ˚
˚ Simultaneously to many things,˙ fully to one: mutually exclusive˙ modes of attention. In a society˙ organized toward the former,˙ capacity for the latter will be˙ difficult to acquire, and practice˙ of it difficult to sustain. ˚ ˚ ˚ ˚ ˚ ˚ ˚ ˚ ˚ ˚ ˚ ˚ ˚ ˚ ˚ ˚ ˚ ˚
˚ Truth as a property of locutions,˙ truth as a quality of relationship.˙ *Can I construct of words and grammar˙ an equal to the world? Can I imagine˙ myself and the other as equals?*
˚ ˚

Voluntary disclosure˙ creates agency, forced disclosure˙ erases it. Poetry, one opposite˙ to torture. ˚
˚ ˚ ˚ ˚ ˚ ˚ ˚ ˚ ˚ ˚ ˚ ˚ Imposed from outside, humility˙ is injustice and oppression; arising˙ from within, it is dignity. How many˙ other virtues display such duality? ˚
˚ ˚ ˚ ˚ ˚ ˚ ˚ ˚ ˚ ˚ ˚ ˚ Does the call for transformation of others˙ include transformation of myself?˙ Exceptionalism, or common cause? ˚ ˚ ˚ ˚ ˚ ˚ ˚ ˚ ˚
˚ Cannot hear others, mishear oneself.

How must I see, to mean what I say?
To love, to articulate one's love.˙ *Can* one do either, without doing both?˙
Or is that what it *means* to articulate˙ one's love: to recognize that until
then˙ one had not loved? ˙
˙ ˙ ˙ ˙ ˙ ˙ ˙ ˙ ˙ ˙ ˙ ˙ ˙ ˙ ˙ ˙ Violence obeys a dream logic.˙ And imposes it.
One logic tested against another˙ sees the other logic as itself. ˙ ˙ ˙ ˙ ˙ ˙ ˙ ˙ ˙ ˙
˙ In how many
senses may one miss˙ a logic? How many logics˙ am I missing, in how
many contexts,˙ right now? ˙
˙ ˙ ˙ ˙ ˙ ˙ ˙ ˙ ˙ ˙ ˙ ˙ ˙ ˙ ˙ ˙ A sequence of associations.˙ Enjoy the results of
association,˙ learn from the principle of association. ˙ ˙ ˙ ˙ ˙ ˙ ˙ ˙ ˙ ˙ ˙ ˙ ˙ ˙ ˙
˙ That we see from a
limited perspective,˙ one aspect at a time, charges poetry˙ to multiply
perspectives, to say "or"˙ repeatedly. ˙
˙ ˙ ˙ ˙ ˙ ˙ ˙ ˙ ˙ ˙ ˙ ˙ ˙ ˙ ˙ ˙ ˙ ˙ Subjectivity assigns value˙ by *coincidence.*
Our divorce˙ was finalized on the very day˙ of the Japanese tsunami.˙ But what
if one denies oneself˙ such associations? (*Can* one?)˙ Is there another
subjectivity? ˙
˙ ˙ ˙ ˙ ˙ ˙ ˙ ˙ Against the society of the spectacle,˙ of ritual display as
voluntary˙ subjugation of individual to group,˙ how can one enact voluntary
self-regulation˙ that does not pretend a unity˙ of individual and collective?
˙ ˙

Over and over Socrates offers˙ his interlocutors opportunities˙ to see that
a question need not *name* me˙ to ask about me. A new definition˙ would
ask whether Euthyphro himself˙ is pious. That question about the world,˙
about the facts or a definition˙ or someone else, may *also* ask how I stand˙
toward the world or my duties or the language.

May one speak only words one already "owns"?
Does nuance differ from detail?˙ Can I give a detailed description˙ that is
not nuanced? A nuanced˙ description that is not detailed? ° ° ° ° ° ° ° ° ° ° ° °
° Immigrant or exile,
seeker˙ or prodigal? Who's reporting, to whom? ° ° ° ° ° ° ° ° ° ° ° ° ° ° ° ° °
° Open form: that openness˙
has many forms, or assumes them. °
° Counternarratives to the war story,˙ and
to the stories of colonialism,˙ patriarchy, expansionist capitalism,˙ racism,
exceptionalism.˙ Education as the offering˙ of existing counternarratives
and˙ of techniques that enable one to create˙ counternarratives of one's own.
° °

"Normal" shifts its valence upon recognition˙ that societal norms *never*
did reflect˙ the interests of a majority, only˙ of a powerful and influential
minority. °
° ° ° ° ° ° ° ° The problem: "my" point of view˙ is always already colonized.
° °

Beyond experience entails˙ beyond understanding. Perhaps˙ understanding
is not so important? °
° ° ° ° ° ° ° ° ° ° ° ° ° ° ° Maybe for some lives a list of words˙ may give the most
apt account? If forgetting˙ threatens human understanding and well-
being,˙ maybe nothing could be more necessary˙ or more human than lists
of words? °
° ° ° ° ° ° ° A phrase from a "small" language within˙ a poem mostly in
English,˙ a phrase from a "major" language (one spoken˙ by a colonizing
nation)? On whom˙ (poet or reader) is the burden of proof˙ placed in each
case?

40

Is it necessity or accident that reduces us to guessing?
How much harder than thinking about a poem˙ it is to think about the
relationship˙ *between* poems, that space that can be entered˙ only by holding
each poem in mind˙ *and* performing the additional˙ operation of comparison.

Lyric poetry not as metaphor,˙ in which one resemblance is contrasted˙ with
the many differences, but as˙ *correlation.* Surely the indicative and interrogative˙
will live on, but the conditional˙ is lost already, depending as it does on a
kind˙ of temporality, a willingness to linger˙ in thought, that lyric poetry
sanctions˙ but "new media" do not. How long can we defer a "real" America˙
with the "new world" of fantasy, of *The Tempest,*˙ the delusional opposite to˙
the illusory enlightenment˙ of the Enlightenment? What difference in self-
understanding˙ results in, and results from, orienting oneself˙ by a map of
the stars rather than˙ a map of the surface of the earth?˙ By a map in which
pattern matters˙ more than shape? Why does the time to weep˙ come first, the
time to ask questions˙ later? Women have had to insist that they can *decide*˙
and *act*; poetry too can decide˙ and act, not only be admired. Who must I be to
have done˙ what I have done? *What* must I be? If I am hidden from life, is life˙
hidden from me?˙ And if hidden *from* me,˙ is life hidden *inside* me?

The fullness we felt did not resemble love, but the emptiness did.
The game is bigger than *any* of its players. Does that warrant despair or hope?

Reorient the chain of being: make metaphysical order not vertical but horizontal.

What cannot be written: what shadow does it cast over what *has been* written?

Why permission to look *out* through windows but not *in*?

How closely can the city come to resemble the country, without forfeiting its pretended right to appropriate the country's resources?

Against the tyranny of fundamentalisms, maybe forgiveness is the one rationality?

Narrative as sequential: one event *replaces* another according to a logic of cause and effect. Lyric as cumulative: one item *adds to* another according to a logic of gravity.

If narrative is sequential, if in it one event replaces another, then in principle it can go on forever. Nothing limits the scope or the size of the novel. But if lyric is cumulative, if one item adds to another, then it has limits, perhaps limits coextensive with my own.

Are obligations imposed by the living always hypothetical and those imposed by the dead always categorical?

As if ruination could speak. As if it gave warning.
That principle or supplement that would make˙ a list more than the sum of
its parts,˙ that would make it *emergent.* ˚
˚ Of the mechanical we recognize˙
that in creating energy it consumes˙ matter. Why not admit that politics˙
transforms humans into its energy,˙ that a nation devours people˙ as an
electric plant devours chunks of coal? ˚
˚ Parsimony demands of science˙ that it
eliminate personification.˙ Why not the same of poetry? ˚ ˚ ˚ ˚ ˚ ˚ ˚ ˚ ˚ ˚ ˚ ˚ ˚
˚ If the regime's
brutality˙ has no limit, can one human,˙ any human, retain agency? ˚ ˚ ˚ ˚ ˚ ˚ ˚ ˚
˚ Perhaps
my project as the reader˙ of a "surreal" poem does not differ much˙ from
my project in relation to˙ the "real" world: to discern the laws˙ according
to which it operates.˙ And maybe the difference is small˙ between what
bearing "real" events might have˙ on my understanding of the world˙ I
inhabit and what bearing events˙ in an alternative world might have. ˚ ˚ ˚ ˚ ˚ ˚ ˚
˚ Does
enlightenment's being the ideal˙ into which we (ought to) seek to escape˙
entail that violence is the real from which˙ we seek to escape? Or might
enlightenment's˙ ideality consist in its contesting˙ the marriage of the
violent with the real? ˚
˚ ˚ ˚ ˚ ˚ ˚ ˚ ˚ ˚ ˚ ˚ ˚ Can one who has known˙ welcome and justice identify˙
with one who has known neither? ˚
˚ ˚ ˚ ˚ ˚ ˚ ˚ ˚ ˚ ˚ ˚ ˚ ˚ ˚ ˚ ˚ ˚ ˚ How ought I live, if what makes dreams˙
counter to the rest of my life˙ also makes justice just? ˚ ˚ ˚ ˚ ˚ ˚ ˚ ˚ ˚ ˚ ˚ ˚ ˚ ˚ ˚
˚ Insofar as it is
decorative, a quilt˙ is organized spatially and synchronically.˙ Its images
and patterns are *arrayed.*˙ But insofar as it is utilitarian,˙ it is organized
temporally˙ and diachronically. Interactions with it˙ are *sequenced.* So too
with a poem?

Is *the age in which I live always the present moment?*
We honor the poor who suffer and die˙ in wars that extend the wealth and power˙ of the wealthy and powerful. Monuments,˙ dedicated cemeteries, holidays.˙ What about the poor who suffer and die˙ *contesting* conditions that secure wealth˙ and power for a few? What places, what days˙ are sacred to their memory?

Perhaps the recondite has appeal only˙ for the privileged, and stating and restating˙ the obvious is important for everyone˙ except those toward whom political arrangements˙ are slanted?

A voice without a face, a face˙ without a voice. Equivalent states˙ for the one who hears or sees them? For the one˙ heard or seen?

My decay: ontogeny recapitulating˙ phylogeny? or fractal self-similarity˙ between myself and my world?

The love poem: I know a private language exists,˙ though I am not one of its two native speakers.

A record of conscience would employ˙ the perpetual present, not the past tense.

Scientific theories of cosmic origins˙ compete to replace one another. Do myths?

Animism doesn't work in science,˙ but is it the whole point of poetry?

You are named for her: you have her strength,˙ and she yours; you have her wisdom,˙ and she your breath;˙ you have her experience, and she your hope.

What we learned of the murder from the position in which the victim was found.
If I can't answer "Where are you from?," I can't say who I am.

Well, then, *you* try to parse the relationship between the spoken and the hidden.

One pool ball striking another, ok, but what about causal interaction *between* the material and the immaterial, the moving moving the moving?

Even given all eternity for the attempt, can the angels who did not rebel ever understand the ones who did?

Memory for the father, imagination for the son.

In the absence of the conditions for meaning, the quest for meaning can only be violent, can only be *violence.*

To Aristotle's insistence that you don't know whether you were happy until after you have died, add: or what your words mean when you utter them.

Poetry's wager is harder than Pascal's. What is to be gained or lost is not a supplementary life but *this* one. If I lose the bet, then the whole of life (perhaps not only the whole of *my* life) was always already meaningless.

A world in which being and meaning stand askew to one another, in which what a thing is and what it means do not match.

No doubt Whitmanian celebration of a singing America never was *possible.* The long shadow of manifest destiny˙ still darkens everything American.˙ Let's not pretend poetry is exempt. ˚
˚ Truth contains one vertically (prevents˙ freefall), and allegory contains one˙ horizontally (prevents straying).
˚ ˚

Activism not preceded by imagination (not able to˙ envision an alternative world˙ and a way to approximate it)˙ becomes war or terror. ˚ ˚ ˚ ˚ ˚ ˚ ˚ ˚ ˚ ˚ ˚
˚ Even superiority to history˙ would not free poetry *from* history. ˚ ˚ ˚ ˚ ˚ ˚ ˚ ˚ ˚ ˚ ˚ ˚ ˚ ˚ ˚ ˚ ˚ ˚ ˚
˚ *Exclamation* makes nothing happen, too,˙ but I don't try to *explain* why I curse˙ when I stub my toe.
˚ ˚

One lives in domestic space,˙ and visits the space of nature.˙ Even "nature poets" maintain˙ the distinction. It would take˙ better charts and maps than we have,˙ to overcome that separation. ˚
˚ If the humanity of humans was global˙ before commerce was, the wisdom accrued˙ prior to the globalization of commerce˙ and technocracy might pertain to lives˙ lived in its wake. ˚ ˚ ˚ ˚ ˚ ˚
˚ A door that does not open is still a door. ˚
˚ The pandemonium of media,˙ the effervescent noise, calls for a poetry˙ that selects and juxtaposes texts that might not meet˙ elsewhere than on the field of the poem, in which meeting˙ and on which field their contradictoriness˙ appears with stark clarity.

QUESTIONS

The right combination of postures to adopt in a holy place?
Why so many poets rehearsing˙ personal experience as anecdote,˙ so few documenting corporate injustice˙ to private citizens? ° ° ° ° ° ° ° ° ° ° ° ° ° ° ° ° ° °
° Is my safety, my not having to face˙ danger or death for my work, merely evidence˙ of my prior erasure? °
° ° ° ° ° ° We have something like a common sense˙ of how events follow one another.˙ But *words*? Does "grammar" function analogously˙ to "cause and effect"? °
° ° ° ° ° If corporate globalization can displace˙ the sustenance economy, why can't I˙ disrupt poetically the pervasive˙ corruption of discourse? ° ° ° ° ° ° ° °
° What does it mean, that "physical discomfort"˙ and "moral discomfort" seem parallel,˙ but "physical pain" and "moral pain" do not? Of which discomfort am I˙ responsible in poetry to give account?˙ Can I account for one by means of the other? °
° ° ° ° ° ° ° What if the poem has no intention˙ of edifying, and no obligation˙ to edify? What if it exists˙ to release me from the moral? ° ° ° ° ° ° ° ° ° ° ° °
° History can have meaning only if˙ it can have *effect*, if we can learn from it˙ and avoid repeating it. What is poetry,˙ if we have not learned, and do repeat? ° ° ° ° ° °
° Are my poetic charges — to enter˙ without reserve into the life and understanding˙ of the other, and to see the other's life˙ and understanding as bearing on my own —˙ mutually exclusive as conditions,˙ and thus paradoxical as obligations? °
° ° ° ° ° ° ° ° Need one have been present in or at events˙ to bear witness?

Can one take anything *seriously without reducing it to absurdity?* Is the making of a list also the telling of a story? Can one distinguish a poem written before 9/11 from a poem written after? Should one be able to?

Is distaste for didacticism merely one luxury of privilege? What if word association *is* a form of thinking, a logic capable, like other logics — math or metaphor — of revealing to us aspects of the world? Is poetry inherently imperial? Does a voice's mattering mean its mattering to the colonizers?

Perhaps one historicizes oneself in part by the insistence with which one contextualizes and recontextualizes historical flotsam, things that have floated away from their original context? Is recognition of one's already playing a role in the drama of war the first element of a counternarrative, as the Socratic recognition of ignorance is the first element of wisdom? Is it a *necessary* element of counternarrative, the *defining* difference from "the war story"?

What are the conditions for valid critique of the language we use to critique things other than the language itself? Absent Socrates' hope that the examined life is worth living, his faith in the redemptiveness — the wisdom — of recognizing one's ignorance cannot stand. Can poetry restore and sustain such hope?

Does poetry have control over any *words?*
To resist, wouldn't one have to bracket˙ the moment of resistance, suspend˙ one's complicity? Is this possible?˙ Or is resistance only a mode˙ of self-deception more subtle than most? °
° What if we hold the mirror up to something˙ besides nature? And what if mirroring is proper˙ to the aural as well as the visual? °
° ° ° ° ° ° ° ° ° ° ° Does orphic-ness release one from, or confine one within, self-expression? °
° ° ° ° ° ° ° ° ° ° ° *Can* one draw inferences about˙ the social and historical from˙ the intimate and personal? °
° Hired mourners. How do I *know* their grief˙ is less deeply felt than mine? °
° Is it *counter*narrative because it tells˙ a different story, or because˙ it tells the story differently? ° ° ° ° ° ° ° ° ° ° ° ° ° ° °
° °Are there not alternatives to the episode˙ as the unit of comprehension? ° ° ° ° ° ° ° ° ° ° ° °
° Does the spatial sense of "before" exclude˙ the temporal sense, if what one is before˙ is the secret of the world? °
° ° ° ° ° ° ° ° ° ° ° ° ° ° Does poetry unsettle its readers˙ because the poet was unsettled˙ already? Or are poet and reader˙ both unsettled by the poetry?

Is not my likeness to a beast more relevant than my likeness to a god?
Does poetry *possess* the property˙ of uncertainty, or *communicate* it? ˚ ˚ ˚ ˚ ˚ ˚ ˚
˚ How
many forms of alienation *are* there?˙ How many can one person endure?
˚ ˚

Does my alienation call into being˙ alienation potential in others?˙ Or call
into action alienation˙ dormant in others? ˚
˚ *A* history could be anonymous,˙ but
how could *the* history? ˚
˚ ˚ ˚ ˚ ˚ ˚ ˚ ˚ ˚ ˚ ˚ ˚ ˚ And what if in the new regime poetry˙ is not
forbidden but impossible? ˚
˚ ˚ ˚ ˚ ˚ ˚ ˚ ˚ ˚ ˚ ˚ ˚ ˚ ˚ ˚ Insofar as vigilance and reason contrast˙ rather
than concur, ought I extend vigilance˙ beyond perception to conceptual
claims? ˚
˚ ˚ ˚ ˚ ˚ Is the counternarrative told˙ by replacing affect with reason,˙ or by
replacing one affect˙ with another? ˚
˚ Is not unsettledness and complication˙
integral to the role of cosmopolitanism,˙ with its implication of being
"between two worlds,'" the global and the local, of relating system˙ to
environment, participating in˙ unsettled and complicated autopoiesis? ˚ ˚ ˚ ˚ ˚
˚ Is this
the claim of lyric, that˙ the world does not *act on* us but *becomes* us?

Imagination that codifies, or imagination that splashes?
What if poetry perplexes and disgusts?˙ Is not a savoring and digesting˙ of experience, but an anorexia? ° Textual signs, material signs.˙ Textual objects, material objects.˙ But textual signs for material objects? ° Can a poem *close* with an *opening?* *Must* it? ° Is locating oneself the same as,˙ or distinct from, describing the features˙ of the world around oneself? ° Is belief that one is repressing something˙ proof that one is not? ° Not the act of inscription but the flight˙ of this moment into the infinite˙ and irrecoverable past. ° Pathos, identification: does one˙ condition the other, or are they˙ reciprocal? Or equivalent? ° Why valorize *identity*˙ (attainment of oneness) over *duplicity*˙ (with its connotations of deception),˙ when clearly society enforces˙ duplicity on some persons by withholding˙ sanction for the identities they would claim? ° Does anonymity alter temporality?˙ Does it make *any* inquiry diachronic,˙ transform taxonomy into history?

Imagination that builds, or that sows?

What would make experience "real" and what would make a poem "real"?
Is it the danger that the two are not identical that necessitates the poem?

What about the fable gives it such force? What about *us* gives the fable
such force? Hieroglyph, or shadow? It makes a difference. Who *am* I when I
read the poem? Is it the combination of linearity and circularity that
distinguishes the poetic sequence from "pure" lyric or story? Or is it the
ironic relation between physiognomy and purpose (outside and inside,
body and soul)? Still a progress, but toward what? Which is on its way? A
state of grace, or winter? How many rules are suspended in a poem that
interrogates poetry? Is the enemy political or spiritual? Without or within?
Shouldn't we ask those questions *before* we act?

Imagination that labors, or that dreams?
Might the truth of the true consist˙ in its susceptibility to self-critique˙ and
resistance to reduction? °
° ° ° ° ° ° ° ° ° ° ° ° ° ° ° ° What does the engagement of form with content˙
have to do with activism? Are they˙ inherently connected, and the task˙
is to *see* the connection? Or is it˙ that they *ought* to be connected, and the
task˙ is to connect them? °
° ° ° ° ° ° ° ° ° ° ° ° ° ° Perhaps not every epiphany is worthy of poetry?˙
And perhaps not every bland observation is unworthy? ° ° ° ° ° ° ° ° ° ° ° ° ° °
° How become
conversant with the other˙ in such a way that the other both is˙ and is not
the other, that one both is˙ and is not oneself? °
° Is the point to make a polis˙
of the cosmos? Or a cosmos˙ of the polis? Is poetry's charge˙ to bring the
world to the city˙ when the city is too small, or the city˙ to the world when
the world is too large? °
° ° ° ° ° ° ° ° ° ° ° ° ° Should I be depicting the world as it is,˙ or as it would
be if there were justice? °
° ° ° ° ° ° ° ° ° ° ° ° ° ° ° Are poetry's limits set˙ by language, by myth, by the
spirit? °
° ° ° ° From what past can voices *not* be channeled? ° ° ° ° ° ° ° ° ° ° ° ° ° °
° Should not the poetic
imagination be˙ (and is it not possible that it be)˙ both sympathetic *and*
analytic? °
° ° ° ° ° ° Ought poetry present what we *can*˙ imagine, or what we cannot?

Which came first, the loss or the lamentation?
If naming can confer identity˙ and immortality, does it matter˙ that it cannot confer life? °
° ° ° ° ° ° ° ° ° ° ° ° ° In a grim landscape, can a portrait˙ be anything but grim?
° °

Within what limits is a poem confined˙ in its invitation to the reader˙ to escape or extend limits? °
° ° ° ° ° ° ° ° ° ° ° ° ° ° ° Is a poem's particularity˙ ultimate, or is its generality?˙ Are we many or are we one? °
° Is *any* progression a "natural"˙ progression? an inevitable one? °
° Why *not* suspicion? ° ° ° ° ° ° ° ° ° ° ° ° ° °
° Even if we are between two worlds,˙ what prevents them from being inscrutable, each˙ refusing communication with the other,˙ or disclosure to its own inhabitants? ° ° ° ° °
° For there to be place, there must be *places*.˙ But does here and there entail us and them? °
° ° ° ° ° ° ° ° Is it possible to cross over, to give˙ here and there a chiasmic rather than˙ a parallel relationship with us and them?

The external world becomes the internal with what inevitability?
Who has the right to speak about war?˙ Its perpetrators? Its victims?
Does anyone *not?* °
° ° ° ° ° ° ° ° ° ° ° In the middle of "telling it slant," can a poet˙ also,
simultaneously, "tell it straight"? °
° Ratio, or substance? Are relationships˙
being identified, or is an essence? °
° If poetry can reconcile us with the past,˙ but
has no predictive capacity,˙ is everything in (and about) it˙ anachronistic?
° °

If poetry helps us choose the path˙ to enlightenment, is it because˙ seeing
the past clearly enables one˙ to see the future clearly enough˙ to see at the
end of which road˙ enlightenment awaits? °
° What if we don't *assume* that a
poem˙ is *really* a song? What if song-ness˙ is poetry's *least* needful quality?
° °

To mistrust and contest my own convictions,˙ to regard poetry as the site˙
of multiple convictions, not subject˙ to colonization by just one.˙ Easier
said than done. How fulfill a decision˙ to be at strife with one's own
convictions? °
° ° ° ° ° ° ° ° ° What fear must be cast out˙ to enter this poem? What fear˙ will
this poem cast out? °
° ° ° ° ° ° ° ° ° ° ° ° ° How articulate an alternative vision,˙ when the vehicles
of communication˙ are part of, and sustain, that to which˙ we need an
alternative?

AS MUCH AS

Night illuminates as much as day.

FIRST ON THE LIST OF DISPERSALS

In these parts, they claim first spot on the list
of dispersals of summer midmorning sunthreat,
those sizzle-silver flares of spray from irrigation arms
satisfying semicircular swaths of corn
defined against thistle and shortgrass and scrub,
and prowled by an impossibly mangy coyote.
Plenty to see in this not-much-to-look-at,
plenty to linger over in this hurry-on-past
where, equally defeated, mortals and divinity
pull toward a more traditional unity.

How hard was it ever to replace a horizon?
Which of us has not already, is not even now?
Why not build our houses into hillsides,
abandon hay bales to rot in ruined water?
I've been cast as a hamshambled barn falling down,
in an uneven field with creeks for crooked seams,
opposite hiveboxes propping one another up,
their dingy white a stage whisper over the meadow's rustle.
In roles more real than themselves, each performs
places and objects that embody our failed dreams.

I trust you to know this as no complaint.
I remember only the *fact* of the movies,
not the movies themselves, projected onto a blank
cement block wall, we tenants all on blankets spread up the slope
or running among those measures, spilling soda.
Childhood as a series of theatrical places.
I remember the gentle tingle in my throat,
the tang on my tongue, of the poison they fogged us with.
Each enspirits the rest of these bright soft insistences,
the loft of raiment transfiguring us.

Where someone shrugged before me, I too shrug.
My window overlooks an intersection at which
a light pole leans in one direction, a stop sign
in another. The streets don't make right angles.
My neighbor mows around a tree stump.
A blackbird blown backward by a rush
of wind reiterates his uniform complaint.
When does, when did, the view forward become the view back?
In that time before this time grown numb to wish,
possibilities skittered within me like neon fish.

NO LONGER THE STRENGTH, NEVER THE COURAGE

Frame, sheetrock, insulate, rewire: we hired done
what I can't do, which is all of it, to transform
into dispersals a garage that was first a barn,
with a horse window that still opens, with walls that,
in hush enough, still whisper what I hear as the shush
of oats and the swish of hay, though who could be sure.
There was a time before cars, and a time
when who could afford them. I feel myself accountable
to keep pure just what proves that nothing ever *was* pure:
a profound awareness of infrastructure.

What I perceive as frenzy I know
has intricate and complicated order.
But what did knowing ever show me that helped?
Wild horses not far from here still stir clouds of grit
when they gallop in loops through the definition
of *windswept*. I *want* to ride the unridden,
but no longer have, if I ever had, the strength to,
and my life proves I never had the courage.
To others it may be, but to me it was not, given
to be aware of both the construct and what is hidden

from the construct. Measure twice, cut once.
I don't cut much, so I've tried to apply
to things I do more often advice that sounds good.
Think twice, speak once. Listen twice, speak once.
Read twice, write once. Not that I succeed. But that barn —
before dawn to hear things that rustle quietly:
mice racing their fear across the hay, the cow's tail
protesting. Sit. Listen, list. Hide within the construct.
Here everything turns white and blows across the highway.
Only when the snow kept falling did I see

my walking speed enforced by a held candle,
know how much more satisfying snow is than sunlight,
hear the half-registered sibilance that measured my sleep.
Sleep twice, dream once. I would ask to dream more often,
but the frenzy frightens me, and feels beyond order.
Is frenzy what separates order from ordering?
Or what takes so much space it shoves them together?
I was getting better at the forgetting we call
dreamless sleep, but with all this wintering
I became an insomniac, remembering.

TENUOUS HOLDS

I want as badly to experience stasis
as to tally progress, to know contentment
as to study hope, all absent accessorizing
with the familiar abstractions: spring, the stars, birds,
brook-smoothed stones, moonlight shimmering on dark water.
May I have, but not take cover under, destinations:
the Prado, Carnaval, the Maasai Mara, Beijing.
We don't all have backyards; let me tend my not-much-of-one,
hear its texture-measured sights, detect what indications
may lie buried within, or beneath, those sensations

that, like all sensations begun as beauty,
end as anaesthesis to loss, augury of death.
Can't lose what I never perceived, can't keep
what I have: one moment of eye contact
with one stranger in one train. Cars in parking lots,
desk lamps and watering cans in windows,
tattered plastic sheeting tangled on barbed wire
and plastic bags bickering with the scrub.
Even transient images prove hard to erase
when I feel I've entered into a place

the way I have into this one whose horizon
is ambiguous: is it the line of mountains
to the west, or the clouds those mountains gather?
At certain times of day, in certain light, one can't tell
which is which, clouds shaped enough like the impacted peaks,
mountains colored enough like clouds to leave me unsure.
As maybe any of us should be always,
and maybe all of us are, admit it or not.
Which will have dispersed tomorrow, which will perdure?
One is always on the way to something pure,

though *always on the way to* entails, of course,
never *at* or *in* the pure thing. It does *not* entail
that one knows what the pure thing *is* that one approaches,
or what a study of its purity might be like,
or that one's progress toward it is steady.
In the interstate median, the sides
of a fallen fifty-three-foot trailer conform
to the shallow ditch, joining other things
in uncertain progress, things with only tenuous holds,
those whippled silos standing silent in the fields.

WHAT CREATURE IN WHAT DARKNESS

So accustomed to light have we grown (evolved, really,
it's not you and me only, not *decision* exactly)
that we forget the lives, species, entire biotas
underground, in caves or tunnels no light tastes, *ever*.
Which doesn't mean they don't inhabit us, or that we
share with them, the horizonless, no traits.
In water the whale, in air the hummingbird:
to these totems I arch elements of identity.
Underground, who knows what sister life-form waits.
I have my library of unconscious states

that I claim awareness of, and accept,
though clearly that's contradiction and self-deception.
What creature inhabiting what damp darkness
will show me what I might morph into, might have been
all this time? Does it glow? What best describes its limbs?
What sounds in what notation by what lurching has it scrawled?
Does it *have* limbs? Does it crawl? Or is it sessile,
gasping then lisping what vagrant spores and molds it may?
Or just *patient*, able to trace but waiting instead, curled?
This is my preferred world, the shadow world

that does not — need not — speak, will not be spoken to.
All this flailing at communication — I'm flailing *now* —
just shows I haven't learned, may never learn, to *abide*.
Who realizes the desperate still wants the needful.
Wait, the subterranean advises. *Wait, wait*.
Because only waiting can measure the gritty
shifting of Patience itself. Even that's misleading, though:
the one who waits despises *Because*.
When she who is here with me is here with me, with me
beneath this city there is another city,

ruins not restored, not even preserved, but hosting
a less demonstrative but equally insistent
other estimation. When she is here with me,
she is the other city, host to (or sum of)
secret othernesses and nethernesses.
We need not think of lives as woven *by a loom*
to think of them as interwoven, and need not pretend
they watch us, or care, to make of them second chances,
alternatives, progress, opportunities to assume
other orientations to the textured vacuum.

IN THE DREAM, A PREMONITION

Except the recurring nightmare in which
a villainous intruder breaks into the house
(I wake up shouting *No!*, which must embarrass Progress),
I seldom remember my dreams. This morning, though,
I woke out of a dream that began with my family
driving toward a horizon (maybe Oklahoma,
maybe Tennessee, but familiar from my childhood),
on a road reduced by snow to an inference from the fence line.
I had in the dream, as in life I have, a premonition
of internal conflicts between identity and persona.

The car was white. We stopped at several farms
(always at farms) to hail relatives, but at the last farm
I was the relative being visited.
We parked beside a frozen pond near a barn.
I stood in the snow nearby, watching *us* pull up.
Daylight measures one of me at a time; this dream dispersed two.
My mother and sister left the car, but the ice sheet's
shivering at their first steps toward me across the pond
made them back up and sit down not to flail through.
And by an indiscernible mixing of old and new

I watched my mother lift me, a toddler, from the car
and shoo me, naked, across the dubious ice
toward that adult me holding out his arms.
Adult me received child me, lay on his back in the snow,
and leaned child me against his bent left leg. I woke
with adult me and child me each staring down the other.
But maybe in recounting a dream I play the role
of thoughtless host imposing family photographs
on innocent house guests. I would never.
They're mostly in the barn now, moldering in a corner,

those photographs, of use now only to nesting mice,
because I believe them no more than I would,
and feel connected to them no more than to,
a picture of Greek ruins. Not one child me in them
returns my gaze. The host of my past selves composes
no civilization from its discontent.
If there can be a private logic, one governs me.
Photographs, barns, dreams, snow-encoded roads. Hell if I know
what of it is, or to whom it might be, salient.
But you can come in here and look around all you want.

TO WHAT LIES BEYOND

This is the time of year when almost every night.
That is no country for old men. Yet once more,
O ye Laurels. My heart aches, and a drowsy numbness.
Such lamentations of the one lamentability
all dread the one dread that we dread to name,
that anyway no name names. He went over the falls
in a barrel, she rowed upstream in a tub.
All any credo ever did is halt a line of thought.
Still, this I believe: there are walls, and then there are walls.
I hope to stage an experience that calls

from within walls to whatever lies beyond them.
(There's *always* a double entendre in "lies.")
"Stage" as in *perform*, but also as in *order*.
Perform for whom, though? *With* whom? Order encoded by
what principle? There is sequence, and then there is sequence.
There is direction, too, though no two please the same place.
I was headed east when my marriage turned south.
Apparently *she'd* measured how sad I was, and how stupid.
Why hadn't I? How tell which way it points, that trace,
somewhere between the critique and the embrace,

that is than bread crumbs less susceptible to birds
but more ambiguous, and than a mushroom
pushed through pine needles hardly more intelligible.
There was a young man from South Philly…
My ophthalmologist swivelled the monitor
to show me color photos of the backs of my eyes,
after a significant-sounding sotto voce *Hmmmm.*
Turns out they're leading the way for the rest of me
through Used To But No Longer to Keep Your Alibis.
Catching in motion the ways the land lies

gets harder as my sight and hearing misprogress.
C-store clerks get nervous when I ask directions
to the City of God. As do librarians when I ask
what world will salvage my world and what for and what from.
With my senses in ruins I can't expect to hear,
but I imagine anyway, and name, what sings
of what is past, or passing, or to come.
It's choral, it's chaotic, it's *ignorant against the sky*,
this convocation, this imbroglio, of blisterings,
some of it complicated, wrapped in wings.

HOW MORE FREE THAN AS IF DEEP UNDER?

Certain measures, like certain names and movements,
present themselves, but we three (here I *presume*
alliance I *desire*) pursue less forthcoming ones,
shapes not given but found or made, shapes of which
the finding *is* the making. Am I wrong to speak of "us,"
to speak *as* us? Or is *that* our comitas,
our acting and speaking as if we shared a soul?
May *I* wander through *your* gardens? May *I* see
as *you* saw, disguising a scanner to pose
as an improvised field camera, moving it close

to peony blossoms, to encode my dread of death?
And what ought we mind (the making *is* the finding)
during summer's long absence, when dessicated stems
turned half-hearted hackles feign fury, when a web
of week-old snow warms the fir? *Makes* it, finds it an outline
that makes of us, that finds in us, a second sight.
But this assertion of their sameness first separates
finding from making. Let me try again. Last motel
I suffered (one of a chain, run down), I hit just the right
time of day and intensity of natural light

to witness, not flowers aflush in fertile soil,
but a man — a boy, really: *that*'s the crucial difference
between genders, that womanhood replaces girlhood
but manhood fulfills boyhood — a boy, then, crossing
the nearly empty parking lot, balancing a broom
on the tip of one finger, maintaining even strides,
and a woman, leaning against a newspaper rack,
smoking a cigarette, watching him walk, hiding a smile.
I doubt we should *want* to know what a balanced thing hides
before it falls. To be caught, to show both sides,

either offers liberation. Not the obvious kind:
bright feathers, wings outstretched, soaring through glinting sunlight,
all that. There is a liberation of *underneath*
to rival that of *above*. A liberation
of *ruins* to match *progress*, of *current* to match *breeze*.
How imagine myself more free than as if deep
under cold water, in the colder water that flows
under cold water? As if. In dread no less
of convocation than of horizon, I keep
out of sight, quiet, but this isn't sleep.

NEITHER PLEA OF INNOCENCE NOR ADMISSION OF GUILT

Certain spills — of oil, of blood — release disaster.
Will it. Yet: water spilling over a falls,
spruce sap spilling amber past ecstatic ants,
snow wind-spilled over fences, salmon spilling upstream.
The spill: cause of saturation, or caused by it?
How better illuminate some other element?
Accept this open letter, accept its sisters, as
my proposal that we might, and my insistence that
we do, *spill*, fulfill as dispersals this arrangement:
balance chance occurrences with intent.

Intent détente, well-meant. Spilled sounds, spilled spellings:
scarred, say, spilled past scared to sacred, secret, secreted.
That's it. I'm ambitious to measure steps to accident,
to court what cannot be courted, color it
coldhot acrylic in what crazy combinations
I can concoct. Primaries, my ass. That nothing *will*
does not excuse, I know, my persistence in
this practice of peculiar surrender
that I know, and anyone can see, *will not* fulfill
my quixotic search for the beautiful spill,

but search I do, for spill I must, as must we all,
not least we who flail toward this gnarled rising, host
its met match as witness attesting to the Attested To.
Think how brightly colored ruin would be, spilling clear
across this black stone, how right its apology
for abandon. Any innocence I pled
would only prove, and exacerbate, my guilt.
Any logic I followed would deceive me, so,
as if against my illness I begged to be bled,
I do not consider sense. Instead,

my left hand contrives trick questions for my right.
Can a shadow *be* a crease, or only encode one?
If a crooked man walks a crooked mile in half an hour,
how long till he reaches the wrinkled colorado sea?
Which, a ton of feathers or a ton of bricks, makes
the more impressive spill? Plenty of nonsense to mull.
Many scents to chase past reason into Into, under
smoke-caked chalk figures crossing patience: weaponed humans,
robust beasts. Convocation enough from which to cull
a novel species, a scaffold. The beautiful.

STAY SECRET, STAY LOST

My understanding that what had to happen had to
did not prepare me to imagine how it would.
What must be is what is not, not what is.
How else contest this paradox than with a liberty —
a libertinism, a spilling — of imagination?
How else prevent the mind's turning territorial
than through such prodigal, even flippant, errancy?
It followed her to school one day, school one day, school one day.
So, against the mind's urge to be imperial,
I am working with random materials:

cherries fallen from the neighbor's apple tree
into my yard, seventy-two sheets from my collection
of page 73s, my grade-school teachers' names, spelled backward,
a vintage plastic model of a vintage 'Vette.
Against the forces out to herdify us,
to standardize our choices by orchestrating
what is offered us to choose from, and thus what and how,
and *whether*, we think, it serves self-definition,
self-defense, to find the unimportant fascinating.
This uncertainty is liberating,

though so would certainty be, as I imagine it
against its absence. Against *my* absence.
That's our straits. The certainty of the certain
has to do no whit with truth, only with mortality.
2 plus 2 equals 4 means only *I can pretend
not to feel my imminent demise, blistering.*
That pretense, in turn, has implications
for the cocksure Hermes in me, measuring himself,
and for the Aphrodite. Ever since he kissed her ring,
she hears voices from the corner, whispering

family secrets she's not sure she ought to know.
Some secrets should stay secret, some losses stay lost.
In my mathematics, numbers would (like horizons)
encode secrets, and sums be thus, like families,
unpredictable. Does this make sense? I hope not:
we became sisters (paradoxically) by refusing
sense its commonness. So, speaking of random,
here's another of the many lies about myself
I hide under that best disguise, a true thing:
the clinking of glasses is musical, soothing.

AND A CODE TO THE CODE

Any event in any *there* occurs also *here*.
Not *repeats* itself here, but *is* itself here.
That human chain protecting protesters in Myanmar:
my actions here join it, or side with the police.
Any event in any *then* occurs also *now*.
That in our language it makes sense to say "fight for peace"
suggests how far it extends, the horizon
of this our flailing through these our ruins.
Still, I insist it's possible to map how serenities
function through systems of fluid affinities,

how they spill through the functions that define systems.
Does yellowing burnish, as in scotch tape or squash?
Or embrittle, as it does the pages of books?
Does history offer language an opposite to *embattle*?
Can we envision *network* as we can *clash*?
To what fugitive interconnections can access
not be denied? Under layers of *regulate*
and *enforce* and *sanctions, suppressions, allegiances*,
relationships fizz, lives adhere and release.
Mapping this ambiguous and effervescent space

studies even what it does not discover,
blisters of meaning, dispersals of order,
a generative delicacy, rebirth of rebirth.
We need not return to a nature we never left.
There's a code here, and a code to the code.
If we broke the one we'd have truth; the other, mystery.
This pond I know, sure all day the birds' songs are beautiful,
but at night, my god, what convocation, insects and frogs.
What winds will be westerly will be westerly
with or without people. History

will end when we do, but not stop. Those westerly winds
will persist without our measuring their persistence.
Thread takes the guesswork from guessing. A stitch makes thread
a map, but a map of what? Any hope is hope
that my map maps yours, is susceptible to stitching.
I neither believe in heaven nor doubt the abyss.
I don't pretend to the capacity for flight
entailed by either, but otherwise I'm ready.
Having in hand a map prepares me to swim across,
not without fear but without hopelessness.

THE SEEN, WINDBENT AS THE REMEMBERED

This place's parchedness does not prevent plasticity of palette.
Spare may not measure up to the splendid: nothing here
rivals your extravagant New England maples.
Still, just yesterday as its substitute my yard declared
a mushroom big as a catcher's mitt, heaped cap upon cap,
orange to outflash any rust flared on any junked fender.
The leaves of the shrub shading it — a stunted tree, really —
fade, veins first, from alfalfa to buttermilk.
I've traded the tracing of tragic consequences for
a primary concern with precise color,

which seems more static only if one insists
that change occur quickly, that consequences follow
within one sitting and enforce a morality.
The cherry near my window encodes a childhood plum
bent permanently — grown — to the east for relief
from wind constant from the west. I trust few tenets,
but the ones I can't defy disfigure me
like that wind that tree. It is, I intuit, possible
to transcend our mundane perceptual limits
a few days at best, and often for only a few minutes

dispersed across a lifetime. Which motivates
our trade in visual — or sonic, or haptic —
equivalents. Show me the tune of your world,
I'll sing you the feel of mine. My working-class wanderings
may never fetch me a glimpse of my old-money god.
God knows what she does in that mansion, what she meant
by these manicured lawns, whether she believes — I don't — in swans
and willows, grazing thoroughbreds glazed by morning mist.
I doubt I could hide dread under an *argument*
for disappearance shading into disembodiment,

but what is this if not that? For my skill-lessness
I compensate with method. To still my flailing,
I haunt ruins, convocations horizoned by hush.
Maybe your swing creaked on ropes from a beech branch, but mine
grated on chains from a rusting frame braced above gravel.
I'm a blister on the knuckle of mortality.
My unhappy childhood mildews in the basement.
Perception spills past and future into the present.
Even in apparent barrenness, when I really *see*
I remember a small ornamental tree.

INELEGANCES

Establishing an interior where before — in the world,
and in me — had been no inner/outer distinction,
windows make me the maker of what makes me,
make the reflection more real than what it reflects,
but also fix inequalities (the light brighter
inside than out), encode the horizon as stasis,
present plot as geometry. Of course most stories simply
leave me out, but in those few that do include me
my role began, and I remain, in medias res,
caught between public and private spaces,

seeing not events but myself as determined by them.
It's a godly power, dividing the greater light
from the lesser, through that comparative measure
revealing imperfections, indelicacies,
interruptions, inelegances. The human power,
maintained by force of will against a moth that won't alight
in the curtains and stay, is to attend, to see
in what is there now what has been, what might be and must.
Godly power to divide creates the human to unite:
sitting before a dark window at night

entails returning to watch frost-stubbled morning sunlight
lurch across the lawn, calling trees' shadows after.
After so carefully structuring an interior,
inviting texture to spill its story to flatness,
listening, in the story the teller does know, for the one
she does not, peeling away from the story its husk
of event to expose its core of image becomes the one
necessary work, one life given to depicting another.
Lives enact their progress and flailing in a musk
unimagined outside: snow gone blue with dusk,

blessed with only one sense, *listens* but cannot smell
what it hears. How stubbornly, though, do I want to stand
behind such distinctions — snow inanimate,
what hushed those tracks into it last night animate? Not very.
Varying that supposition turns on a light inside,
gives the window to give me not the world but a reflection
of the room, its colors and textures, and myself in it.
Reflection, after all, tells a story and *is* one,
with backdrops like those in Renaissance portraits: I mean
wild foxes, stiff with seeing and being seen.

BETWEEN ANY TWO FLAT WORLDS

Though the world be flattened that we visit when we visit
a world of ink across paper, so is the world we visit *from*.
What dimension we experience, we experience
only in — *as* — what separates the two flat worlds.
Who still pretends to depth, still thinks to find it
by looking *in* rather than *across*? Who believes
any more in "objectivity," much less in the "real"?
Who would not prefer, does not solicit, the *un*-
observable, unnamed convocation that outlives
human characters in these obtuse narratives

that tell what our world is like by their unlikeness to it?
It's one of the puzzles for us, we whose attempts
to juggle achieved only vexation from our mothers
over bruised oranges, who were not fast or strong enough
to be in position to make the mistake of intercepting
a fourth-down pass. (*Fourth down, knock it down.*) It explains
nothing, childhood. I shot a .22 and missed a squirrel.
So what? We'll never elevate nostalgia to history.
The same memory that loses teachers' names retains
ladders, mazes, bells, and paper airplanes,

displays them as museums display Asian folding screens,
Islamic miniatures, a bronze-age axe head into whose
patina from its inset stones the soul has migrated,
and medieval European book illuminations.
All those craftspersons and monks and slaves and copyists,
liberated from, liberated by and into, what they made.
For no other life would I exchange my own, surely
because I feel gratitude, but maybe, too, because
I lack imagination. How would it measure up, to trade
the parchment look of the background, yellowed and frayed,

to what I experience as the looping and spilling
of what I would call my life? How different are
those loops and spills at 33 than they were before,
at 78? If a loop's a loop and a spill a spill,
then a trade might be progress, or ruins. My youth
for my age, my life for yours, a twenty for two tens.
After exchange, next question: on what would *giving* depend?
What *does* separate, what would join, our two, any two, flat worlds?
To whom can I will my dispersals, lacking heirs and assigns?
One barely there, little more than a hint of lines?

WISPS FOR MORTAR, TRACES FOR BRICKS

I don't want to fix against the horizon *anything*,
even what I've loved, even by encoding as ruins
everything, all of it good, all of it gone.
Morning sunlight on the house across the street,
erasing seams from its white siding. Emerald shimmer
of a black feather, twirled in my fingers, that sunlight crazes.
I toil at the opposite of building, at measure
that contests structure, at a masonry
not of mortar and bricks but of wisps and traces,
assembling insect collections and creating secret spaces

for ephemera, labors lost to profit but urgent of grace.
A chip of bark whose underside records the path
of what, a worm? a wood-boring beetle? its larva?
A shard of green sea glass, its edges tumbled smooth.
A lavender sachet bound with a slender lavender ribbon.
As if gathering to myself enough nonsense,
rearranging it with enough care, returning to it
often enough, would populate absences, mollify longings.
Whose curiosity suffices, who has enough patience
to make sense of the world and its mysterious events?

Whose arrangements replicate the reticence to which
they attest? Surely we know better now than realisms
or picture theories. Surely the shadows of leaves
on the dust grains, remnants of rains, scattered countless
across the window glass tell us that, tell us
everything gone *is* good. But are we prepared to hear?
If all the gone is good, and all the here already gone,
don't I have to affirm that everything here is good?
Lacking ambiguity, how could a message be clear?
When activating the stasis is the eye the ear?

When making shoebox dioramas is the hand the eye?
Shouldn't it be? A vision can be dread or steady.
I see someone looking in at the window,
I hear someone listening in at the door.
My home insists I learn, teaches me how, to hurry;
my travels illustrate instead how I might dwell.
I took what I took when you gave what you gave.
I saw what I saw when your assurances shushed me.
Sight is kelp animated by surge and swell,
sound is an invertebrate swirled in its metal shell.

DRAWN FROM, LEFT BESIDE, POURED INTO

"Landscape" misrepresents what represents both earth and sky,
"figure" misfigures what mediates between the two.
I prefer "archive" and "performance," "fog" and "enthralled."
Or "facing" and "effacement," "awful" and "awed."
It's hard to hold a pose, any pose, that does not encode
as dread my irrelevance to the composition.
No two opposites — body and soul — merge in me;
instead, a unity stands opposite, itself to itself.
One of me listens, one watches, for those long lone
moments when earth, sky, wind, and human presence are one.

While I wait for the next, I try to name the last,
knowing naming futile when the named cannot rejoin
the convocation, knowing myself no God-charged
Adamic namer able by pointing to reify,
authorized by any utterance to measure.
We humans never were alone in bearing a face meant
to speak and be spoken to, though each of me finds
the other's expressions perplexing. Guess, and guess again.
Whether I look through a lens or through a casement,
I am never sure about my placement

against a horizon of mountains that disperse clouds
and clouds that spill out mountains. These buckets of light,
did someone else draw them just now from the river,
or were they brought here to its banks, left for me to find?
Having found them, am I supposed to pour them in?
I ask because it's a *river*, and will not expand
no matter what I pour in, no matter how fast I pour.
Note the recurrent theme of my uselessness. Had I been,
when one was needed, a prophet, I would have warned:
we who rose up out of the open wound

blistered from self-doubt into the one hushed into ruins
sometimes cannot maintain distinctions between
mirror and window and lens. So we call "aperture"
what offers enclosure to open space, and the reverse.
I learn later what in the moment I never know:
which one of me an exposure is exposing.
I will return at this time tomorrow because
I saw here at this hour yesterday what I seek:
a study, that progress against progress, composing
on its shoulders a thing so large it weighs nothing.

THIS BODY A SEA

She wrote what she wrote. Her digging dug her out
of *Dark down here and hard to breathe* into *Bright enough*
to turn my stomach, gotta squint, can't tell where I am.
Can't tell what season this is supposed to be, can't guess
what sort of storm is likely, what species of bird
might be migrating through. Can't decide who to tap
for what advice until I know what ruin threatens.
I have the feeling of being watched, but not watched over.
It doesn't faze me that your mind is difficult to trap
because it lives in a strange region. There is no map

that does not encode the strange, and no map
that *does* locate the hush at the source of the spill, name it
what its natives name it. If I name it first,
will I then recognize it when I see it?
Or must the naming wait? I've blistered this long.
Does the region's being strange make strange the oceans
that surround it, or is it made strange by their being stranger?
If names don't measure here what they measure there, do numbers?
That was the decomposition of lessons
and this is the invention of questions

such as: Is there a one-to-one ratio
of lakes to clouds? Who would know? Who keeps count?
To whom ought it matter? Because I can drink the water,
I know not to call this body a sea, but it's wrong, too,
to name it a lake when it makes the horizon.
Tell me again how to distinguish switch from brome.
One of them stretches farther behind me than this water
stretches before. Through one of them a man is walking.
Room after room withdrawing, out of room,
gloom out of gloom uncoiling into gloom:

that's how he described what he described when he thought
he was warning me, but not what I saw when I went
where he told me not to go, the whole time asking myself
the question he forbade me to ask anyone
I should pass along the way. I passed no one.
The strange is stranger to the partially blinded
than to the partially deaf. As a girl displaced
and excurrented, I postulate that flailing
dislocation, unconfigured and unkinded:
a boy as a place but disorderly but minded.

THESE UNDERWATERED

If even thumbnails bear me messages —
your blood is borrowed but the bruises yours to keep —
then where am I, and who? Was my disappearance
spilled to the authorities before I learned of it
myself? I could know I have gone missing
only by report, but where would they send the delegation?
Where *did* they send it, that it never arrived here?
I can't quantify my location. I can neither
interrogate nor represent my fascination
with forms of interrogation and representation.

Or is it that I can interrogate *only*
interrogation, represent only representation?
Toward a hushed horizon, toward blistered ruins:
is one progress so different from the other?
I know you are telling me something your words are not,
but I can't connect your posture with your intonation.
You are to me an ocean, beyond governmentality.
What good has it done me (read: what good *would it do*)
to understand that there can be no purification
of knowledge, power, subjugation, and mediation?

How does it help to know that power *is*
power of subjugation? The subjugated must measure
what the powerful need not. There's still above the wreck
a slick to mark the spot at which it sunk,
though the leak turned long ago from news to history.
We stood gun together, he and I, for a year
aboard a ship we hoped would stay invisible.
Now we stay ashore, where gales blow crows backward
instead of gulls. Even if, as I fear,
we've not been here long enough to disappear,

they may have been here first — am I wrong to fear that too? —
and taught themselves to disappear us. Who says I can't choose
for my ambition the ambition to go missing?
By what agency, into what convocation,
am I being encoded? I hadn't known my longing
to be a neverbeen until I knew these underwatered,
I hadn't guessed the burnlessness of rope sliding through my hands,
the indifference of oil's silent rising to the slick, until
I lost those days defending the hemmed against the tattered,
nights pretending the dead never mattered.

NOT WHERE I LOST COUNT, BUT WHEN

Sculptural works serve also as drawings, songs
also as autumn afternoons. Ceramic vessels,
spun to perfect circularity, stand, such measured
testaments to so many lives lost, so much time past.
Only tragedies are only themselves. That year
house finches hushed us, nesting in the holiday wreath,
we had to use the back door even for guests.
All these mysteries — handwritten letters from strangers,
trunks in attics, weather and argument, music and math —
create variations of tone, density, path,

variations spoken of but not spoken, or spoken to,
encoded as dread, blistered into the old brain.
Years as markers worked fine until I lost count.
But that's what I want, not the unit, leaf by purple leaf,
but the accumulation, the adding up that adds up to
a losing count, sum not arrived at through addition.
Day by day my days became not days, as my breaths
long ago became not breaths but respiration.
I take as our stay against decision
the outer reaches of our peripheral vision.

I frequently return to the fact of return,
follow the verb to the noun. I frequently
figure the figure, distrust distrust. Less often,
I wander along the lakeshore, trying to measure
whether this my pretense of progress is still, and is for me,
just because it was once, for someone else, a path.
When I pass the boat this path spills past, I wonder
how long ago and for whom it last was a boat.
Let me claim this as my measure of your stealth:
you are in between the lines that have no breadth,

on a plane with no depth, yet you have the dimensions
of blood, thread, and wire, the tone of that handwritten letter.
Even peripheral vision has limits: colors
in autumn convocation, yes, but what about the smells
dispersed along the path? What about the lakeshore
I never wandered, the boat I never rowed, as a girl?
I don't remember where I lost count; I do remember when.
In my last life I learned only specific gravity:
she floated, I sank. But here — you, me, second life, second world —
we can see we are stone and we are burl.

LOOPED AND SPOOLING THINGS

I like it here above the weather, or above
the changing of the weather (since by "weather" we mean
that changing), here where cold is colder than dark is dark.
Think of the things whose measure could total
to the height of any height: rope, electrical cord,
ribbon, tape, the bracelets and necklaces and shoestrings
she left behind when she left everything behind,
never mind the scarves or the strands in her hairbrush.
One flies south for winter, another sings,
trying to recognize the force in things

that have no force of their own, whose force is the force
of combination, that progress, in defiance
of math, toward convocation other than sum,
a whole too restless for equation with the all.
Before I'd been here, I knew this place as the place
above weather, where the weather stays surprising,
as only constancy could in this our world of decay.
Things to loop or tie, things to thread or spool:
I afford all my studied sentimentalizing
not by changing them, but by recognizing

their already being what I would ruin them into.
Never mind the scarves. All that dread, that hushing
before the ornate and the majestic earned us
a few horizons lit jack-o-lantern orange,
and the fantasy that autumn and sunset bring peace.
I know I can't influence weather, but why not try?
Why not sum a few looped and spooling things,
find out what, in combination, they enforce.
The principles of spill are hard for blister to defy.
The snows fall slow, as if the world were an eye

open in sleep. Which I for one take it to be,
because my own most familiar sensation
is of observing one world from another,
decoding the rules of the one but bound by those
of the other, able to learn *of* but not learn *from*.
Where there might come a storm, it feels dangerous to play
by the rules of sunshine. But could I reach up,
I would stretch toward the vacant, to which I whisper.
Unless I check the forecast, I feel lost all day.
Could we hoist ourselves above this weather, would we stay?

AS IF IT MEANT TO THEM WHAT IT MEANS TO US

Then it was gone. The one truth I've ever spoken.
The one prophecy I've made that always comes true.
I watch others' watching, to see what they see
and how they see it, though I know from the watching
that I don't see it, can't see it, as they do.
Still, it helps to find in others' visions sources
for one's own seeing, to hear in "medium" not only
"technological means" but also "diviner."
It's always the old ways the new ways enforce:
snapshots taken from the network of cameras

monitoring weather and road conditions,
the weeping of one driver, the drowsiness of the next.
Who wouldn't get drowsy, driving this measure of the dark,
who wouldn't weep? Who wouldn't spill the same stories
over and over? Who wouldn't come to believe them?
Who wouldn't learn to whisper the hush of petitions?
I was born to it. I know what to petition *for*,
though not who to petition *to*, so I know
what to say, but not whether anyone listens.
I search through the randomness to find compositions

to rival this night encoded on this windshield.
Dispersal wants progress toward disappearance, toward gone
beyond the movement of harsh weather or the stillness
it imposes on us, gone to the horizon
where space collapses into time. Or vanishes
the way flocks vanish into mist, or herds
into fog or snow. *Why not* illuminate
an empty parking lot, the yard of a dark house?
They outline the history of failure, my words,
at the same time blown-out tire fragments like awkward birds

blister the interstate's shoulder, and in the same way.
We treat other travelers as if, like us,
they traveled to get *themselves* one place to another,
as if "destination" meant to them, as it means to us,
home or lover or family funeral, not warehouse
or transfer point. Which of us does travel *not* make a ghost?
And those blurs that cross, rather than following, the highway:
do they inhabit our world, or only visit it?
It's hard now not to think we only *seemed* to outlast
small figures illuminated briefly as we passed.

CAREFULLY SELECTED DEGRADATIONS

The more I am promised, the less I expect.
The more secure the reasoning, the more I wonder.
The more self-sustaining the object, the harder I work.
Now that I sleep alone, I don't sleep. Every sound —
the house settling, rustling in the leaves — becomes footsteps.
Treatment is a science, but my illness needs an art.
Once I learned I was ill, *everything* became
a symptom, even my efforts to prop up my health.
All my intricate (and no doubt overwrought)
intuitive and ritualized strategies are part

of a larger plan code-named "Passing By and Wondering."
None of it is original, but that doesn't prevent
its being personal to me. If not with these spilled crumbs,
how am I to encode my enforced disappearance?
Who has any but borrowed presentational means?
One need neither miss nor mistake the horizon
to mismeasure it, misattribute to it
all manner of music and moans and mutterings.
Though we join in chorus to intone what we intone,
geomorphic relationships stand alone

and stay insistently silent. Even to say
they listen would be to pretend *our* obligations
apply to *them*. They don't *do* anything
on a time scale we can comprehend, or with a form
of agency that resembles anything we flail toward.
They're saints alright, but not a sort we can anoint.
And there are various sorts: ones who protect us,
ones who fight in our places, ones who give succor,
ones who suffer only extremes, so as not to taint
the physical pain in their lives. Twitch response. Trigger point.

Saints suffer public crises as their blistered lives.
Our guilt or anger they take on as *their* progress.
I'm less noble, unwilling to assume the role
of scapegoat through my own agency, but neither
do I wish to join the convocation of free riders.
I don't fear the hunter, but I do fear the trap.
I don't fear the journey, but I do fear the vehicle.
Degradations can be small and carefully selected.
We *ought* to be astonished when things overlap.
Look at the dry needling, look at how big the gap.

A FALLING THING ON FIRE FROM ITS FALL

Ruin and renewal. If I must expect the first,
how orient my life toward the second?
What does hope look like — *act* like — when it is not idle?
Through what window onto what other world may I look
for an alternative organization of space,
a reconstruction of the possibilities of home?
I don't sleep well anymore. While I listen to mice
in the walls, in the kitchen, encode my disappearance
as their skitterings, I flail toward the question: How come
the legibility and erosion of form

depend on but resist one another? Why must
painting defy architecture? What was
that earthward streak of light? From how high must an object
begin its descent, to catch fire from its fall?
What kind of falling thing can burn without burning up?
I prefer a dim, history-lit freedom
to such phosphorescence. I doubt we need, and I'm sure
we can't survive, much streaking across the sky.
To transform my spills into progress, I try to rhyme
observational studies, developed over time,

with spontaneous, dispersed experiments
meant to surprise laws whose operations we can't see.
That something is colossal does not make it permanent.
Give me entanglement, and you can keep grandeur.
The built loses to the improvisational.
Its being impossible does not make vain
an attempt to redefine the dominant powers. Meanwhile,
I listen for, and listen to, all things mathematical:
root and tentacle, tilted city, mill and machine,
subjects in the golden light of the golden mean,

all followers of formulas for frenzy.
Any landscape has many layers, whether or not
more than one shows, so my work is archeological:
it blisters even hidden layers, those longest buried.
In youth, my orders always were to *listen up*.
Now, horizon-pressed, I study how to *listen here*.
Opposites, to be opposite, must share measure.
It's hard to distinguish pursuing prey to hell
from following a pilgrim to finisterre:
the tonalities belong to the same register.

SUNK UNDER, BURSTING FROM

One hears the gender admonitions from one's past
and elects whether or not to heed them:
if only it were so simple, like stepping outside,
while coffee brews and one's lover sleeps,
to bring in the paper. The lover's implicated,
as is the news, even the coffee. What looks like *scene*
is also *plot*, what feels psychological may be spiritual as well.
Am I lonely, or am I lonely and desolate?
God knows why I persist in trying to *explain*
a flattened and simplified picture plane.

I know I ought to stop, hush, linger, study, dwell,
but that demands measures of patience and trust
I don't possess. It's easier to state than to ask,
easier to be Euthyphro or Theatetus,
even Aristotle, than to be Socrates.
A smoking room would be a convenient place
for intrigue, that inconvenient but, well, *intriguing*
pastime of those with means for it, spare rooms and idle hours.
Give it two figures and *any* still implies
striking narrative and figurative overlays.

Any horizon enforces mine, any story
tells my story, or at least foreshadows
what ruins this progress of these events encodes.
I'm fascinated by the luminous nimbus
that hovers over convocations. I want one for myself.
Instead, I'm visited — harried — by headblind losses,
ill-fitting blouses, badly stitched, missing buttons.
That my urge for knowledge left with my hope for it
I took as permission to content myself with guesses:
coffee, tea, chocolate, silk and spices,

cement-encrusted wheelbarrows, a rust-blistered stroller
sunk under weeds beside a spill-bent bike,
birds bursting from and burrowing into ivy
overgrowing a brick wall, or even — the birds —
clinging momentarily to still-exposed mortar.
I trust dramatic tension. Without permission
from either, I disappear into the argument
between the wound and the healing, from which
I've learned to pursue an art of inflammation,
outside of the luxuries of decoration.

FIRST HUSKS, THEN SHATTER

My practice is to become alert — more and more
alert — to the ironies and pretenses
and complicities of practice: this practice,
any practice, in such convocations as ours, in which
I pretend alertness is possible, would be progress.
The more complex its syntax, the fewer
will be the speakers of a language, and the broader
its horizons of kerning and scale, blister and hush.
The more bird-like its imagery, the harder to lure
painting into the space of the viewer,

who may be deciduous instead of avian,
limited to a single flight, really a respite,
dizzy and elegant, from the business of a fall.
On this fragile surface, these fugitive materials
will enforce on my spills first ruin, then disappearance.
Should I care what catastrophe takes structure from?
On aluminum or paper, hidden or staged,
information encodes other information.
Its mimicry is also mockery of the sublime:
it cannot be viewed completely at a given time.

First I hear the husks, and only then the shatter;
first I see source, and only later measure;
first trophic cascade, and only after that tailings.
Deformation exhales other deformation,
detritus attracts, and occasions, more detritus.
That a muscle cramps involuntarily
does not diminish the pain it sponsors.
That corruption is legislated does not purify it.
Consider your reflection/position warily.
Choose your direction/devotion carefully.

No point in our pretending, either of us,
not to be one teacher of those classes
enrolled with boys, naked to the waist, who learn
to scavenge landfills for screws and circuit boards,
who feed their families by fending off the gulls.
On all the sun-blinding places, the ice shelves
and snow-bound islands, our ancestors died out
generations ago. Here in warm regions we insist
on building, though no one any longer believes,
our cumulative monuments to ourselves.

AS IF WE WERE, AS IF WE WERE TO

I create lozenges compacted from listenings-in.
I illuminate familiar dreads and hushes,
fit their formal structures to unique objects.
I badger abstractions into relevance,
assign names to otherwise anonymous sufferings.
I make things to study, though I make them *from*, selfishness.
Each passing train shifts keepsakes on my walls and shelves.
Though I myself don't want, I do want others to want,
more dialogue, more complex argumentation, less
imagery and narrative. Artifacts of process

are artifacts in progress toward ruin: the handles
of the china teacups out of parallel,
the sepia photos askew. Photos of whom?
I buy whole boxes of them at flea markets,
frame them, enshrine them on one wall in convocation,
pretend them my ancestors, as everyone pretends,
no matter how their photos came to them.
The photographed whisper to one another. I listen in.
I obey what my body, not my conscience, commands,
act only on what is happening under my hands

and *to* them. What *grounds* have you to distrust fidgeting,
deny it wisdom and measure? I might look better
corseted, but loosen those stays — look out!
I'm pink and wild. I have hair where you've never seen,
and won't until you lie to me, give me beads
and baubles, paisley scarves and velvet wall hangings.
I love (and thus demand) *that* you give; I don't care *what*.
And you, my animal, my pet, do I love more
your party-colored artificial fur, or your stuffings?
We are no longer young but still sprout wings

as if we were. As if we were, too, of a species
fit for flight, encoded by the thousand generations
that preceded us to fly before the snow
to a spill of flowers, and after it to return
to meadows and marshes and perpetual sun.
Is it my memory or imagination that teems
with associations my old life put into place?
My hairbrush and my thicketed reclusiveness,
my tablecloth and my failing, flailing, snowblown schemes,
my apartment and my unsettling lavender dreams.

BETTER OVER THAN ACROSS

Quilts and rugs: scraps worried into convocation.
For my grandmother, it wasn't a hobby:
she wanted her children warm at night, *she* wanted
to be warm. They couldn't afford to buy what they could make,
or to buy two of anything. Grandfather with his one
good arm had one good suit, on which Grandmother would sew
patches when it had holes. Same for her one good dress,
and for each child's one school outfit for the year.
This wasn't just her; it was her whole generation. Although
they didn't call themselves artists, they did what artists do:

scavenge and transform, recontextualize
and reconfigure, effervesce and incandesce.
All the meaning we *intend* and *plan* and *design*
is derivative meaning, but that makes it also
historied, charged by and full of what preceded it.
To understand any work, look for the indications
of those quilts. But look, too, *outside*. Measure
records movement, movement activates measure.
They are one another's study and ruins:
seasonal change, tidal flow and migrations

of birds and butterflies, caribou and elephant.
All those quilted acres across North Dakota
and Nebraska, all those children spilled from Swedes
migrated generations back. But now what?
Absent transitivity and completeness,
absent subtractive processes, what horizons
excite them to follow the flyways, winter otherwhere?
Do any still migrate — flocks, herds, exiles — except
through my sleep? Dream butterflies, dream elephants:
without demarcation, these ghost-shaped whites with their translucence

are, instead of *leaving*, letters to hushed relatives,
letters to flailing trees and places left behind,
letters scrawled as fossil skeletons dispersed across
page upon page in sedimentary stone,
not written to be read, but still written.
The world we blister in need not be the one we mimic,
nor the one we migrate through the one we map.
I say better to go over than across.
The less we have, the less our urge to take.
How much we make, how much we need to make.

NOT TO RECORD BUT TO REMARK ABSENCE

I've stopped trying to *secure* my beliefs:
let them drift, let them teeter precariously.
Instead of having, and participating in, structure,
let them be emanations, essences
susceptible to representation but not
corporeal, not susceptible to breach
or dispersal, essences given to color
rather than to figure and outline as their proxy.
Let me imagine, intuit, research,
and interpret an actual aura for each.

Let those auras be real as memories, vivid
as dreams. Why shouldn't I see better in sleep?
What obliges reality to present itself
only to my waking mind, in material form,
and in the same way it shows itself to others?
If the subject glows, let the portraitist
paint hue and saturation. Let figure follow
as it will. If identity may be layered
and composite as ruins, its hush will be enforced
through color, an emotional presence surfaced

without structure, in defiance of edges.
It's true we've gotten good at measuring,
but measuring can't salve our ache for the measureless.
Work how hard we will to claim the dry and bright,
hold out our arms against what landscape we choose:
neither relieves dependence on, neither absents us from, dream,
in which one horizon touches the other.
Nothing outside the law but nothing visible to it.
No childhood impatiences and loneliness but became
noses against the window, no steam

except the steam of human breath, which does not record —
too fugitive for that — but does remark absence,
dread, anticipation, wistfulness, flailing hope.
It wasn't bedtime stories that spilled me into sleep,
but my parents' conversation in the kitchen.
To this day it's not aria that soothes me but séance:
words whose implications I need not understand,
from voices I recognize, absent but nearby.
Studious encoding, convocation of disappearance:
things form above the definite evidence.

STACKED, LAYERED, HUSHED

Why take the opacity of the opaque
as a limiting limit? Why not instead
as a defining limit, a conditioning one
that encodes into openness the closed, enforces
the reappearance of figures hushed under sediment?
I believe in the capacity of surface
to blister even what chafes far beneath it,
but I *trust* its capacity to distort and transform.
Possible or not, I make it my project to displace
many traces of time, multiple dimensions of space,

the various layers that, stacked, codex memory.
I study, I measure, ordinary things
to demonstrate that nothing is ordinary.
Familiar, maybe; ordinary, no.
By imposed, chronophotographic layering,
I seek to distort and radicalize perception,
to recognize as convocations of love and dread
these cut flowers browning on a windowsill.
In addition to addition, it takes precise registration
to form a personal visual accumulation

of possible experiences that reveal
the actuality of actual experience:
only lined up just so do they show that, and how,
they do not match. What surfaces is not
surface itself but what flails up from below.
It is not hope that hopes, nor grief that grieves,
nor wind rousing its leaves that spills this tree's voice.
I save the book I found half-buried beneath it,
though long ago it was ruined by rain, because *it* saves
what had been done there in the shadow of the leaves

by people I cannot know, but whose lives I repeat.
Instead of a diary of events, the book
held a list of sibilances, sonorities,
celestes. The first rain, that chastises fallen leaves,
the second, that hushes them. The hisses
and whispers those same rains elicit from the highway.
Things seldom progress as we expect. It was not the *tree*
that succumbed to a sparrowriddled listlessness.
The humans all left for the place of worry,
but the tree stayed behind to whisper her story.

Human proportion need not occur at human scale.
Human duration need not equate to human span.
So when I fill a field the size of myself
da-Vinci-outstretched, I suffer no illusions
about beauty and truth, about outrunning death.
The organic disperses, and often spills, the cancerous.
Which of us does not consume more than our desert,
replicate ourselves faster than we can be consumed?
Out of my contingency and your chaos,
highly-wrought, decorative elements coalesce

toward a convocation defined by organicism
but not itself organic. One sensuality
measures what adds, another what multiplies.
Yes to constant-temperature pools in limestone caves,
but *Omigod* to stream beds desperate with spawning salmon.
I dread that moment, the identity of suspense
and fragility, toward which who does not progress.
I know things were together, once they fall apart.
The more complex and blistered the order, the more tense
with the threat of disunity and incoherence.

The broader the domain of the legislation,
the vaster the ruins left over, left behind.
Power cannot outlast the outlyers, and doctrine
could only overlesson them. Ours *is*
the planet of cats, furtiveness the one virtue.
Expect swift moves, sudden attacks. Expect no arbiters.
Here anything not withheld must be hush-encoded.
Here any least breeze enforces the duress of duress.
The judge needs suspects, the warden needs prisoners.
There is no scarcity of noiseless interlocutors

in ceremonial garb from whom to receive
command, or of vociferous ones constantly
issuing commands passed tyrant to tyrant
since the age of bronze. In those days tyrants
in exchange for merciless slaughter sponsored beauty.
These days they still slaughter but we get only lies.
The servants at court and the concubines hold the place
of the last word but do not fulfill its function.
Made immodest by the presence of such spies,
I undressed myself in front of ornamental eyes.

TOWARD A CONVOCATION OF EPHEMERA

The length of my list of good intentions measures
less my generosity than my ineffectiveness.
Others progress, I flail. Malice doesn't often
weigh against my virtue, but torpor does.
Torpor, and the inability to respond
that follows from inadequacy of vision,
an inadequacy that funds my ambition
toward a convocation of others' ephemera.
Lacking it myself, I admire the hard-won,
other people's intentions to get things done,

their faith in what work can do, their persistence in its doing.
There's nothing except illusory hope to pluck
from the lowest-hanging branch in my yard, a live-oak limb
bigger around than any two of me, that has leaned
perilously since before I was born. I have
less to say in favor of ease than in praise
of apparent inconsequentiality.
What do we add to the ruins but what we hardly notice?
Grain by grain, the accumulating sorites,
evidence of human commitments, tastes, priorities,

grows inadvertantly, a testament we wrote,
keep writing, are writing now, but don't know how to read.
Not all of it — not much of it — good. It includes
"byproducts," "garbage," "collateral damage," "side effects."
Whatever we hide, euphemize, deny, repress.
How will we respond, if our representations
of catastrophe falsify causation, plead not guilty?
We need ways to refigure, to *see* again
the disappearances enforced by our prior calculations,
expand our gaze beyond its current margins,

its horizon defined by yield, by p/e ratio.
A grocery list written on a paper plate
(*rice, mustard, ice cream* — what was its author planning?)
or a solitary imperative (*Return shirt!*).
In either case, the unlikelihood of *anything*
individual underneath the decadent,
impersonal, franchised corporate megalith
encodes in ephemera their hush. Never mind
that none of us are any longer innocent,
fragile traces of the individual are resonant.

CONSTANT, MODEST, ANONYMOUS

Is the encoding as memory of event
progress into ruins, or disappearance?
Honeysuckle does not grow only where
it is welcomed, but it does make the yard
thick with butterflies and heavy with scent.
We who are anonymous already need not disguise
ourselves or our intentions. Who would be deceived?
To whom would the deception matter? And yet:
how describe this study, than as an attempt to surprise
specimens of previously unknown butterflies,

those brilliant exemplars of anonymity?
If a butterfly spills from shade into sunlight
when no camera is near, are its wings colorful?
If I recall a back yard from my childhood,
what enforced horizon must it cross to return?
Will the memory, like the yard itself, host
butterflies? Will they still dust my fingertips?
What is it if not butterflies I watch for
here where the climate is measured and modest:
temperate in the central valleys, with cloud forest

higher up the slopes. Light breezes, warm days, cool nights.
One fallen tree trunk, it seems, for each shallow pond,
always with the rootball exposed, always
with an algae mat on the water merging
with the moss hushed on the trunk. Eagles fish this stretch of river,
nest in this stretch of canopy, pass one by one
across this stretch of sky. Deer forage in the undergrowth.
Lichens, mushrooms, orchids unique to this hillside:
each convocation adapted to a single zone
within the rules of the sublime. Images own

neither the landscape nor what moves through it,
though they, and we, may try, ought to try, to own up
to both, embrace both kinds of saturation:
in which all defines, and is defined by, the horizon,
and in which magnetism gives orientation.
After I'm seduced, I want to classify:
give me a definition of love that trains
the attention more intently on the beloved.
What does this much color — so bright, so saturated — imply
in a landscape the size of your eye?

LAVENDER THE GREETING, THE CLUE

Full disclosure: it's not the number of selves
I fret, but their instability. Two, three,
what the hell. But which is which? And does one of them,
any one, study itself long enough to *be* itself?
If I return home to a sprig of lavender
inside the screen door, is that enough information
to tell me a friend dropped by while I was away,
or might the visitor yet have been a god?
Why not measure my dread, count it a dispensation
to use intuition and imagination

to extend the horizons of analysis
beyond cost and benefit. Extend them how, though?
By enforcing nevermindness or justincaseness?
By disappearing into lessonlearnedness?
Dispersing notquiteness, ofcourseness, afterallness?
What if I don't admit the futility
of my blisters? What if I stop counting to ten
before I let myself cry? Maybe instead of structure
and function, wandering and informality
combine to illuminate a reality

worth pausing over. I don't mean a dog napping
on a June afternoon, and I don't mean boys and girls
in yellow t-shirts swarming a soccer ball.
Or deer at dusk hushing from woods to cornfield.
Have you *seen* them? Doing anything but *bounding*,
they're clumsy, those graceful creatures. I hate to waste
all these encoded things, signs a prophet would read
if we had one. I'd read them if I knew how to prophesy.
Of course when I flailed out "I'm lost, I'm lost, are you lost?"
nobody answered. I need to mind what matters most.

I need to answer others' needs, as I need others
to answer mine. Pareto optimality
was never optimality enough, nor did
Arrow's impossibility theorem rule out
what it ruled out, nor Borda's rule bind those it bound.
Against the statistical I want a *moral* norm
of reciprocity in prodigality. I want
the reticence of inelasticity
and its insistence. You are the blood, spilled warm
on the sharp end of the conversation. I am the form.

FISTFOUGHT

Listen closely, and the measure still resonates:
the engine's repeated octave through each gear
as the last truck accelerated away
from the loading dock, taking with it the last shipment
of the last goods from this warehouse, loaded by its last
laborers. Flail as we might against the event
with all its beer-soaked, fistfought consequences,
all its holes in plaster and lath, a time comes
when a building no longer means what it meant.
The overlooked and forgotten urban environment

needs, therefore, to be recorded *and* interpreted.
Maybe others want a legacy in cash; I'll take mine
in trowel and hod, blister, plumb line and flux.
Though I'm not sure what, or who, any legacy is for.
I still have recordings of sounds I overheard
on long walks decades ago. But what to do with the tapes?
Like old warehouses, they were made to outlast
their maker, but already they're progressing toward ruin, almost
as fast as I am. Each enforces the other's time lapse.
I focus on aged and damaged cityscapes

to help me remember how corrupt my memories are.
What more blatant effort have we yet made
to *last*, to be sturdy and indestructible,
than all these factories and warehouses?
All that *brick*, in strict convocation. Detroit, Cleveland.
It's an inelegant truth, but insistent,
that nothing we build lasts. So why she and I
thought *we* could defy it remains a mystery.
Each of us mistrusted the other's intent.
I asked for a kiss. She asked for a testament.

I hoped to help her feel at home, and hoped
she would reciprocate, but home meant one thing
to me, and something else to her. That testament,
I didn't finish it until the kiss had ended.
By then, already, we stood a house divided,
both of us arming for the secession
she had declared. That was one storm that showed me
a few porosities I hadn't known to dread.
Propose a theory if you want, send a delegation:
a liquid's most obvious attribute is repression.

IN PLACE OF ONE RUIN, ANOTHER

If the world set spinning on the axis of my cane
at each hushed step included even one person
beyond myself, it would not dizzy me so.
I lived before you were alive and before my first death
in a house with wooden mantels, intricately carved:
columns, guilloches, pastoral scenes in relief.
But they followed the furniture into the fire.
Hunger and cold rank heat higher than art.
I dread all horizons: not only the grief
but also the beauty of the last years of life,

dispersal or disappearance, strictly enforced.
My steps now are studied as those of a doe
through ankle-high marshwater near a meander.
Are stars still stars if they constellate on the river?
I don't mind the slowing down, it's the uncertainty:
those last steps were shallow, but always the next may be deep.
The choice came, to keep a tidy house or keep the cats.
I can't bear even the thought of living alone.
I measure gravel and sand into a paper cup
to express a feeling of confusion about hope,

though — what the hell — my confusion extends
to everything I care about or feel I ought to.
I've become already the last thing I'll become ever,
one of the identical shingles mushy with moss
arrayed over rotting timbers on the steep slant
of a barn's roof. Maybe it was always so, but now haste
happens to me, is not something I can choose.
If I anticipated one ruin, another came.
Forest fire, winter storm, industrial waste.
Mud, curb, sandy road. Give up living like a ghost,

I told myself. Choose between the truths all choose between.
The truth of low-hanging clouds that winter here
in convocation as if there never had been sun
and would not be, or instead the truth of compound eyes
in artificial light reflecting back the whole spectrum.
I *listen* to my fatigue. It says weaklings
flail the door back and forth to circulate the air.
It says the plan to replace water yet may work.
Never mind the burning tires, the uranium tailings.
The plums are fattening again. In the pond the ducklings.

SURFACE EFFECTS

Text overlain on it transforms a face into
an expression; a face underneath it transforms
text into a poem. So we inscribe on bodies —
I on yours, you on mine — descriptions of selves
we imagine haunting them. All the expressions
that before we knew to read the poems we must have missed:
we *did* miss them. Or mistook them. And in mistaking
others' expressions of course mistook our own.
It is the overlay, not the face, through which we invest
thoughts and feelings, sometimes spoken, sometimes suppressed,

with even the possibility of legible affect,
as if they were true, as if anyone else
shared them, could share them, would even want to.
So I enhance color, focus, and surface effects
on the face second, on the overlay first.
I call it rational to flail and blister, spill and enforce.
From what principle should I seek exemption?
Is there any truth except the human gaze?
We measure our steps, grow cautious and precise
at a threshold we are often reluctant to cross,

but what if it's safety we're protecting ourselves from?
What I dreaded, I waited for; what I waited for was one
with the waiting; not so with what I crossed over to.
My departure, at night and on foot, was a disappearance
to the place of textless faces, where no convocation lasts.
That's the kitchen knife, this is the lily.
I've enhanced of the one its glint, I've overlain
with chasing the other, to mimic its petals' veins.
Silence times its arrival infallibly.
The usual white hush permeates the gallery,

highlighting embarrassment and fear, those moments
of solidity and color. Each emerges
like a massive animal coalescing out of fog,
imposing on the mist its vast aspirations, the shush
of one leg's shag against another's at each step.
Or emerges with another kind of imposition:
in human form but ghostly and unencoded and gaunt,
moving through the gallery *and* through those of us in it.
Because her expression is blank and pale and drawn,
today it looks to me as if her face is my own.

AS ENERGY, SO ITS FLOWING

Improvisational travel: how did it happen
that something once commonplace, almost obligatory,
can disappear, even become unimaginable?
When did we begin to enforce progress, come to need
identity between the hush we leave *for* and the spill
at which we arrive? When did *dizzily*
stop being praise? Are we the same people we were
if we prefer tethered to windblown and adrift?
Contesting, as if one could contest, entropy,
my desire is to capture the flowing energy,

to gather from it what it has gathered
from its pass through order, to make other order
of the encoding, the encoded, and the spent.
If I cannot be one through whom the energy flows,
let me be one before whom it passes.
As energy has meant, so its flowing will mean.
Let me manage many listenings-in, all licit,
all leather across wood, all rustle of shirr and taffeta.
Clean and intimate, intimate and measured and clean,
a fluidity that would otherwise go unseen,

a hitchhiker traveling where he is taken,
accepting rather than claiming space, embracing
gift in preference to plan as his source of direction.
What ought to come of movement if not grace?
What ought to come of grace if not beauty?
What energy flows through beauty if not the secret,
sunrise sent out from me now, then, always?
Is it motion I love, or blister, motion's residue?
Here in the world of energy, a dancer's grace drawn tight
functions as rope or wire, and the arcing streaks of light

replace what our material selves study as structure.
What resists explication may welcome embrace,
but may demand deference or insist on mystery.
Remember that in our passing over this earth
we cross the thinnest crust, beneath which all is molten.
These dancers defy laws, disperse rather than obey
those — gravity, inertia — that bind the rest of us
to our acquiescences, our holdings-back.
They flash toward what outglints result: red and gray,
impetus and tether, as well as wind and spray.

HUSH, GLOW

Here's what all those ruins were for: the encoding
of memory into flame, scars through burn into blister.
Love, though no louder now than it ever was, is molten.
What dread I study, I study by its light.
I hear it without seeing it, feel it without touching it.
Of all the lessons I learned from the infernal,
most important was not to trust any lesson given.
Listen for, and find behind it, the lesson it withholds.
I took this from what was offered by the diurnal:
what lies between the ephemeral and the eternal

lies, as do the ephemeral and eternal themselves.
Which leaves us where, who tell ourselves we want the truth?
What is this language I flail toward but do not speak?
Things whispered, but not *only* things whispered, stay secret.
There is no equivalent of equivalence,
no report back yet from a below below the below.
One brevity given gives one brevity back,
the aftereffects of the aftereffects.
May I not *choose* what all of us were born into?
Absorption and evaporation, light and shadow,

dispersal and convocation, fire and storm.
Had I chosen another *time* at which to let go,
I could have chosen another *way* to let go.
Without wanting to know what the questions are,
I say yes to the first, no to the second.
It's not leaves themselves that mimic flame, but their turning.
One I call an accident, two a story,
three pattern, four a myth. Five I call kindling.
Through, and after, an enforced unlearning,
the memory retains the process of the burning,

correlative in the mind of bodily disfigurement,
the traces and the tracing, the moltenness
and its hiss across the surface it remeasures,
immediacy and residue, sizzle and hush.
First glow, then smolder, then survey your own disappearance.
Of burning, I trust what the fire disbelieves.
From burning, I seek to preserve what the fire consumes.
To burning, I yield what the fire already owns.
Of burning, I celebrate what the fire itself grieves:
the line of ash and ashen images it leaves.

ABOUT THE AUTHOR

H. L. Hix lives with the poet Kate Northrop in the mountain west, in an 1880s railroad house, and writes in a studio that was once a barn.

Books from Etruscan Press

Etruscan Press Is Proud of Support Received From

Wilkes University

Youngstown State University

The Raymond John Wean Foundation

The Ohio Arts Council

The Stephen & Jeryl Oristaglio Foundation

The Nathalie & James Andrews Foundation

The National Endowment for the Arts

The Ruth H. Beecher Foundation

The Bates-Manzano Fund

The New Mexico Community Foundation

Drs. Barbara Brothers & Gratia Murphy Fund

Founded in 2001 with a generous grant from the Oristaglio Foundation, Etruscan Press is a nonprofit cooperative of poets and writers working to produce and promote books that nurture the dialogue among genres, achieve a distinctive voice, and reshape the literary and cultural histories of which we are a part.

etruscan press
www.etruscanpress.org

Etruscan Press books may be ordered from

Consortium Book Sales and Distribution
800.283.3572
www.cbsd.com

Small Press Distribution
800.869.7553
www.spdbooks.org